P9-ARV-420

Fashion

Titles in the Discovering Careers series

DISCOVERING CAREERS

Fashion

Ferguson's

An Infobase Learning Company

Discovering Careers: Fashion

Copyright © 2012 by Infobase Learning

All rights reserved. No part of this book may be reproduced or utilized in any form or by any means, electronic or mechanical, including photocopying, recording, or by any information storage or retrieval systems, without permission in writing from the publisher. For information contact

Ferguson's
An imprint of Infobase Learning
132 West 31st Street
New York NY 10001

Library of Congress Cataloging-in-Publication Data

Fashion. — 1st ed.
    p. cm. — (Discovering careers)
  Includes bibliographical references and index.
  ISBN-13: 978-0-8160-8056-4 (hardcover : alk. paper)
  ISBN-10: 0-8160-8056-9 (hardcover : alk. paper) 1. Fashion—Vocational guidance—Juvenile literature. I. Ferguson Publishing.
  TT507.F338 2011
  746.9'2—dc23   2011021502

Ferguson's books are available at special discounts when purchased in bulk quantities for businesses, associations, institutions, or sales promotions. Please call our Special Sales Department in New York at (212) 967-8800 or (800) 322-8755.

You can find Ferguson's on the World Wide Web at
http://www.infobaselearning.com

Text design by Erik Lindstrom and Erika K. Arroyo
Composition by Erika K. Arroyo
Cover printed by Bang Printing, Brainerd, Minn.
Book printed and bound by Bang Printing, Brainerd, Minn.
Date printed: October 2011

Printed in the United States of America

10 9 8 7 6 5 4 3 2 1

This book is printed on acid-free paper.

CONTENTS

Introduction

You may not have decided yet what you want to be in the future. And you don't have to decide right away. You do know that right now you are interested in fashion. Do any of the statements below describe you? If so, you may want to begin thinking about what a career in fashion might mean for you.

____ My favorite class in school is sewing.

____ I have a good sense of which colors go together, and which do not.

____ I like to use my hands to make or build things.

____ I work hard to make my school reports attractive.

____ I make posters for my church or school.

____ I enjoy photography.

____ I often visit malls.

____ I make my own clothes and jewelry.

____ I like to suggest fashion looks to my friends and family.

____ I enjoy putting outfits together.

____ I like decorating my own room.

____ I spend a lot of time using art and illustration programs on my computer.

____ I enjoy drawing.

____ I like to look at fashion magazines.

____ I am interested in colors, shapes, and textures.

Discovering Careers: Fashion is a book about careers in fashion, from Costume Designers and Fashion Models, to Fashion Photographers and Tailors and Dressmakers. Careers in fashion can be found on runways, in factories, in retail shops, in newsrooms, and in art studios. Some Fashion Designers create work that is considered art, while others design fashions that are functional and are meant to be worn. While the fashion capitals of the world might by Paris, France; Milan, Italy; New York, United States; and London, United Kingdom, people around the world are interested in looking good and wearing clothes that make them feel attractive. Fashion workers allow this to happen.

This book describes many possibilities for future careers in fashion. Read through it and see how the different careers are connected. For example, if you are interested in modeling, you should read the Fashion Models chapter, but also read about Fashion Designers, Fashion Models' Agents, Fashion Photographers, Makeup Artists, and Photo Stylists. If you are interested in sewing, you will want to read the chapters on Apparel Industry Workers, Costume Designers, Knit Goods Industry Workers, and Tailors and Dressmakers. If you like writing, you should read the chapter on Fashion Writers and Editors. Go ahead and explore!

What Do Fashion Workers Do?

The first section of each chapter begins with a heading such as "What Buyers Do" or "What Personal Shoppers Do." It tells what it's like to work at this job. It describes typical responsibilities and assignments. You will find out about working conditions. Which fashion workers design clothing? Which ones work at computers in offices? This section answers all these questions.

How Do I Become a Fashion Worker?

The section called "Education and Training" tells you what schooling you need for employment in each job—a high school diploma, training at a junior college, a college degree, or more. It also talks about on-the-job training that you can expect to receive after you're hired, and whether or not you must complete an apprenticeship program.

How Much Do Fashion Workers Earn?

The "Earnings" section gives salary figures for the job described in the chapter. These figures give you a general idea of how much money people with this job can make. Keep in mind that many people really earn more or less than the amounts given here because actual salaries depend on many different things, such as the size of the company, the location of the company, and the amount of education, training, and experience you have. Generally, but not always, bigger companies located in major cities pay more than smaller ones in smaller cities and towns, and people with more education, training, and experience earn more. Also remember that these figures are current salaries. They will probably be different by the time you are ready to enter the workforce.

What Will the Future Be Like for Fashion Workers?

The "Outlook" section discusses the employment outlook for the career: whether the total number of people employed in this career will increase or decrease in the coming years and whether jobs in this field will be easy or hard to find. These predictions are based on economic conditions, the size and makeup of the population, foreign competition, and new technology. They come from the U.S. Department of Labor, professional associations, and other sources.

Keep in mind that these predictions are general statements. No one knows for sure what the future will be like. Also remember that the employment outlook is a general statement about an industry and does not necessarily apply to everyone. A determined and talented person may be able to find a job in an industry or career with the worst outlook. And a person without ambition and the proper training will find it difficult to find a job in even a booming industry or career field.

Where Can I Find More Information?

Each chapter concludes with a "For More Info" section. It lists resources that you can contact to find out more about the field and careers in the field. You will find the names, addresses, phone numbers, and Web sites of fashion-oriented associations and organizations.

Extras

Every chapter has a few extras. There are photos that show fashion workers in action. There are sidebars and notes on ways to explore the field, fun facts, profiles of people in the field, and lists of Web sites and books that might be helpful. At the end of the book you will find three additional sections: "Glossary," "Browse and Learn More," and "Index." The Glossary gives brief definitions of words that relate to education, career training, or employment that you may be unfamiliar with. The Browse and Learn More section lists fashion-related books, periodicals, and Web sites to explore. The Index includes all the job titles mentioned in the book.

It's not too soon to think about your future. We hope you discover several possible career choices in the fashion industry. Happy hunting!

Apparel Industry Workers

What Apparel Industry Workers Do

Apparel industry workers produce, maintain, and repair clothing and other products made from cloth, leather, fur, or synthetic, or human-made, fibers.

The first step in making a garment is to take a designer's original model of a garment and make a pattern out of it. *Patternmakers* make these patterns, usually with the help of a computer. The pattern indicates cutting lines, buttonhole and pocket placement, pleats, darts, and other details. Computers also grade each pattern piece so it can be used for several size garments. Now the pattern is ready for mass production.

Cutters spread out fabric on cutting tables and cut material by hand or using machines. A cutting mistake can ruin yards of material, so cutters must be very careful.

Cut pieces of cloth are prepared for sewing by *assemblers*. Assemblers

EXPLORING

- Visit Career Threads.com (http://careerthreads.com) to learn more about opportunities in the field.
- Read books about sewing.
- Visit the Web sites of schools that offer programs for apparel workers. The American Apparel and Footwear Association offers a list of approved college programs at its Web site, http://www.apparelandfootwear.org.
- Visit a clothing factory to observe the machinery and activities that go into making a garment. Try to talk to some of the apparel workers to gain insight about their jobs.
- Work on a fabric project yourself or join an organization, such as 4-H, that offers such projects.

DID YOU KNOW?

Where Apparel Industry Workers Work

- Large and small manufacturing plants
- Laundry and dry-cleaning businesses
- Retail clothing stores

gather the various pieces needed for each garment, including lining, interfacing, and trimmings. They match color, size, and fabric design and use chalk or thread to mark locations of pockets, buttonholes, buttons, and other features.

Sewers make up 70 percent of all apparel workers. They use machines to sew together the loose pieces of fabric. Hand sewers may do work that is too exact to be done by machines. Since a variety of sewing operations and machines are required for each garment, workers are classified by the type of machine and specific product on which they work. Workers are categorized into those who produce clothing and those who produce non-garment items such as curtains, sheets, and towels. Here are a few of the typical job titles for workers who operate machinery: *textile knitting and weaving machine setters, operators, and tenders; shoe machine operators and tenders;* and *textile cutting machine setters, operators, and tenders.*

After the sewing operations have been completed, workers remove loose threads, basting, stitching, and lint. The sewn product may be inspected at this time.

Pressers operate automatic pressing machines. Some pressing is done as a garment is assembled; sometimes it is done at the completion of all sewing. Delicate garments must be pressed by hand.

Apparel inspectors and *production control technicians* monitor all stages of the production process. They keep materials flowing smoothly. They detect defects in uncut fabric and semi-finished garments. They may mend these defects themselves or send them back for repair. Inspected finished clothing is then sent to the shipping room. From there, the product is shipped to stores.

A garment factory is a bustle of activity as workers go about their various duties. (Ric Francis, AP Photo)

Tailors and *dressmakers* make garments from start to finish. They must know about all phases of clothing production. Tailors typically focus on creating clothing for men. Dressmakers create clothing for women. *Custom tailors* and *dressmakers* take measurements and help the customer choose fabrics. Many tailors and dressmakers work in retail stores, where they make alterations and adjustments to clothing.

Knowledge of fabrics and their characteristics, as well as good eye-hand coordination and the ability to perform repetitious tasks, is necessary for apparel workers. You should also be able to work well with others, accept direction, work well on your own, and be willing to continue to learn throughout your career. Knowledge of computers and electronics will be increasingly useful as the industry becomes more technical.

Education and Training

Few employers of apparel workers require a high school diploma or previous experience. However, courses in family and consumer science, sewing, and vocational training on machinery are helpful. Since computers are being used in many areas of production, knowledge of them is also useful. You should earn a bachelor's degree if you want to work in management in the apparel industry.

Earnings

The apparel industry is highly competitive. Low profits and wages are common. According to the U.S. Department of Labor (DOL), the average annual salary for apparel industry workers was $21,580 in 2008. The DOL reports the following mean annual earnings for apparel industry workers by specialty in 2009: patternmakers, $39,010; tailors, dressmakers, and custom sewers, $26,640; sewers, hand, $23,030; and sewing machine operators, $20,260. Many workers in the industry are paid according to the number of acceptable pieces they turn out. Therefore, their total earnings also depend on their skill, accuracy, and speed. For example, a worker who produces quality garments quickly will earn more than a worker who is not able to make as many garments as fast.

Fashion Glossaries on the Internet

- Apparel Search Main Glossary
  http://www.apparelsearch.com/glossary.htm
- Dress King Fashion Glossary
  http://www.dressking.com/search/glossary.htm
- Kohls.com Glossary of Fabric & Fashion Terms
  http://www.kohlscorporation.com/ecom/valueadded/Glossary.htm

Outlook

Employment of apparel workers is expected to decline rapidly in the next decade. Increased imports (apparel that is manufactured in other countries and shipped to the United States) and a heavier use of labor-saving machinery will reduce the demand for these workers. Employment will be slightly better for tailors, dressmakers, and custom sewers, but job opportunities will continue to decline. Apparel industry workers who have been cross-trained and are able to perform several different functions have a better chance at keeping their jobs during periods of job decline.

FOR MORE INFO

For information on the latest fashion market trends and news in the industry, contact
American Apparel and Footwear Association
http://www.apparelandfootwear.org

For career information, visit
Career Threads
http://careerthreads.com

Buyers

EXPLORING

- Get experience in the retail field. Apply for a part-time job at a department store, boutique, or other retail shop.
- Explore door-to-door sales opportunities. Girl and Boy Scouts often organize sales drives to raise money for local troops. Your school might also need volunteers to help sell gift-wrapping paper, wreaths, cookbooks, or other goods to raise money.
- Talk to a buyer about his or her career. Ask the following questions: What made you want to become a buyer? What do you like most and least about your job? How did you train to become a buyer? What advice would you give to someone interested in the career?

What Buyers Do

Buyers select and purchase goods that are sold in local and chain stores. Buyers often specialize in one kind of merchandise, such as clothing, jewelry, or toys. The goal of all buyers is the same: to find and buy the best products at the best price for the store or chain (a group of stores owned by the same company) that employs them.

In some stores, buyers are responsible for both buying goods and supervising the selling of goods. In other stores, they are involved only with buying.

All buyers must be experts in the products they buy. Buyers order goods months before the store will sell them, and they must be able to predict how many will be sold. To do this, they must know all about the product—what it is used for, how well it is made, what it looks like, and who will buy it. Buyers must also know the best sources for purchasing the product.

When they make purchases, buyers need to have a clear understanding of what type of merchandise the store owners prefer. For example, some store owners want to sell a large number of lower-priced goods, such as inexpensive shoes or knit caps. Other store owners prefer to sell a smaller number of higher-priced goods, such as designer jeans. Buyers must clearly understand how much profit the owners are trying to make. This will help them determine how much risk they are allowed to take in the type and quantity of products bought. If large quantities of goods do not sell, the store loses money.

A successful buyer must also understand what the customers are looking for. Buyers must stay up-to-date about what kinds of goods are popular, how much their customers can afford, and at what time the customers prefer to buy them. Buyers need to know the sizes, colors, and other features that will most satisfy their customers' needs.

Buyers often supervise *assistant buyers*. These workers spend much of their time maintaining sales and inventory records.

Tips for Success

To be a successful buyer, you should

- be organized
- have excellent decision-making skills
- understand and be able to predict the tastes and buying habits of consumers
- have good marketing skills
- be willing to travel for your work
- have strong communication skills

Education and Training

Most buying positions require at least a high school diploma. In high school, you should take courses in math, business, and English.

Although college is not always required to become a buyer, you will have a better chance of getting a job with a bachelor's degree. If you go on to college, take courses in business administration, communications, fashion merchandising, marketing, retailing, purchasing, and economics.

Earnings

A buyer's earnings will depend on his or her employer's sales volume (the amount of a product a store sells). Mass merchandisers, such as discount or chain department stores, pay among the highest salaries.

The U.S. Department of Labor reports the median annual income for wholesale and retail buyers was $48,650 in 2009. The lowest paid 10 percent of these buyers made less than $29,000 yearly. At the other end of the pay range, the highest paid 10 percent earned more than $88,000 annually.

DID YOU KNOW?

There are many other career options in the retail industry outside of working as a buyer. Following are a few of the main career paths in retail, according to the National Retail Federation:

- Distribution, logistics, supply chain management
- Entrepreneurship
- Finance
- Human resources
- Information technology and eCommerce
- Loss prevention
- Marketing/advertising
- Sales and sales-related
- Store management
- Store operations

Outlook

Little or no change is expected in the number of jobs that will be available to buyers. Many businesses are merging, which results in the blending of buying departments. When this happens, people with overlapping job duties are often laid off. Big companies are also getting rid of buying departments at local stores and creating one central department that handles buying for all the company's stores. This also creates fewer jobs for buyers. In addition, the use of computers, which speeds up business processes, will contribute to fewer new jobs for buyers. Some job openings will result from the need to hire replacement workers for those who leave the field.

FOR MORE INFO

For career information, contact
American Purchasing Society
PO Box 256
Aurora, IL 60506-0256
630-859-0250
http://www.american-purchasing.com

For career resources, contact
Institute for Supply Management
PO Box 22160
Tempe, AZ 85285-2160
800-888-6276
http://www.ism.ws

For information on purchasing careers in the government, contact

National Institute of Governmental Purchasing
151 Spring Street
Herndon, VA 20170-5223
800-367-6447
http://www.nigp.org

For information on educational programs and careers in the retail industry, contact
National Retail Federation
325 7th Street, NW, Suite 1100
Washington, DC 20004-2825
800-673-4692
http://www.nrf.com

Color Analysts and Image Consultants

What Color Analysts and Image Consultants Do

Color analysts and *image consultants* help people look their best. Color analysts assess their clients' coloring, including skin tone and hair and eye color. They teach them how to use their most flattering colors in clothing and makeup. Image consultants usually work with people in business, helping them present themselves in a professional manner. They help clients work on their overall appearance (including office dress code consulting and business casual dress) and grooming. They help them improve their voices, body language, and etiquette (manners). Consultants also may coach clients on dealing with the public and the media. Some may even do personal shopping for busy clients.

Color analysts and image consultants work with individuals, for professional or social organizations, or for all the employees of one company. Others work with department stores, teaching salespersons about color and style and presenting in-store workshops.

Many people in this field own their own businesses. This means that they have to do everything necessary to make their business successful, from advertising and marketing, to invoicing and other office management tasks, to the actual color analysis and image consulting.

Education and Training

There are many classes in high school that will provide you with the basic skills that you will use as a color analyst or image

EXPLORING

- Read books and magazines about beauty and fashion. Local and community libraries should have books on color, fabrics, style, etiquette, and body language.
- Talk to color analysts and image consultants about their careers. The Association of Image Consultants International offers a list of consultants throughout the country at its Web site, http://www.aici.org.

- Get together with your friends to experiment with different clothing combinations and makeup styles.
- If you are in high school, try to land a part-time job selling clothing or cosmetics in department stores, working at a beauty salon or spa, or in any other setting that allows you to interact with the public.

consultant. For example, take English, speech, and drama classes to help you develop your communication skills. Art classes are also helpful to take, especially classes that teach color theory. Since many people in this line of work are entrepreneurs, consider taking any business, bookkeeping, or accounting classes that will give you the skills to run your own business.

There are no formal training programs for color analysts and image consultants. Many aspiring workers attend seminars or classes on color, psychology, training methods, and communications. Others participate in informal apprenticeships with experienced analysts and consultants. They gradually gain experience and are able to eventually start their own businesses. Many image consultants enter the field after working in the business world, and have degrees in management, communications, or business.

Earnings

Earnings for color analysts and image consultants are determined by the number of hours they work, the type of clients they serve, and their geographic location. Color analysts and image consultants earn salaries that range from less than

Helping Hands: Lindsay Giambattista and Taylor's Closet

Simply donating bags of her unwanted clothes to girls in need was not enough for 14-year-old Lindsay Giambattista. Instead, she reached out to family and friends with her desire to help others, particularly girls her own age, and from there Taylor's Closet was born.

Today, Taylor's Closet—named after Giambattista's deceased sister—offers free, new clothing to girls in the foster care system in Florida, as well as those who have left the system after reaching the age of 18. Every month, girls are allowed to come to the "store" and choose up to six items, many of which would be priced out of the girls' limited budgets in a regular store. The new designer clothing, ranging from trendy jeans, hoodies, and blouses, has been donated by popular stores.

News of Giambattista's project spread throughout the community, prompting many retailers, designers, and the public to give clothing and accessories, and make monetary donations. Support has been so great that Giambattista was able to build a larger location for Taylor's Closet and help set up sister stores throughout the country. Taylor's Closet currently has a new project—the Bundles Program—that hopes to reach even more girls by sending bundles of clothing to those in need in other communities. Girls can also take advantage of the many classes offered at the store. The classes teach life skills, sewing, cooking, art, and discipleship.

For Giambattista, the success of Taylor's Closet is not as exciting as the positive changes in the girls' attitudes. New and fashionable clothing allows these girls to "fit in" and prompts them to have a better attitude about their future.

Sources: Associated Press, Taylorscloset.org

$20,000 to more than $75,000. Those who own their own businesses might make far less than $20,000 when starting out. Very successful entrepreneurs (business owners) can make more than $100,000 a year.

Outlook

Overall employment of personal appearance workers is expected to be excellent during the next decade. Opportunities should also be good for color analysts and image consultants. Many people are becoming concerned with how their personal looks and style of dress affect how they are viewed by others—especially in the workplace. They are seeking the services of color analysts and image consultants to help them stand out at work and, if they are out of work, during the job search. Despite the good employment outlook for color analysts and image consultants, it is important to remember that these occupations are small. It will be a challenge to land a job or build a business from scratch.

Tips for Success

To be a successful color analyst or image consultant, you should

- enjoy working with and helping people look and act their best
- know a lot about fashion, style, and etiquette
- have a friendly outgoing personality
- have excellent communication skills
- be able to offer constructive feedback to clients
- be professional at all times
- be willing to work hard to build your business

FOR MORE INFO

For information on image consulting, contact
Association of Image Consultants International
100 East Grand Avenue, Suite 330
Des Moines, IA 50309-1835
515-282-5500
info@aici.org
http://www.aici.org

Costume Designers

EXPLORING

- Join a school drama club or a community theater. Volunteer to work on costumes or props. School dance troupes or film classes also may offer opportunities to explore costume design.
- Learn to sew. Once you are comfortable sewing clothes from commercial patterns you can begin to try making some of your original designs.
- Read books about costume design.
- Practice designing costumes on your own. Draw sketches in a sketchbook and copy designs you see on television, in films, or on the stage.
- Talk to a costume designer about his or her career.

What Costume Designers Do

Costume designers create the costumes worn by actors in plays, on television shows, and in the movies. They also design costumes for figure skaters, ballroom dancers, and other performers. During the planning of a show, costume designers read the script. They meet with directors to decide what types of costumes each character should wear for each scene.

Stories that take place in the past, called period pieces, require costume designers to know a lot about what people wore during different historical time periods in different parts of the world. For example, in the course of their careers, costume designers may work on movies, television shows, or plays that are set in the Old West, in ancient China, or in Europe during the 1700s. Designers conduct research at libraries, museums, and universities to study the garments, shoes, hats, belts, bags, and jewelry worn by men, women, and children.

They look at the colors and types of fabric and how garments were made. Even for stories that take place in modern times or in the future, costume designers might use ideas that come from looking at the details of historical fashions.

Tips for Success

To be a successful costume designer, you should

- have excellent artistic abilities
- have good sewing, draping, and patterning skills
- be able to work well with others
- be flexible regarding design changes requested by your employer
- have basic illustration skills
- be able to work under deadline pressure

Once they complete their research, designers begin to make sketches of costume ideas. They make these sketches on paper or by using computer-aided design software on a computer. They try to design each outfit to look authentic, or true to the time period when the story occurs. Designers also pay attention to the social status of each character, the season and weather for each scene, and the costumes of other characters in each scene.

Costume designers meet with directors for design approval. They also meet with stage designers, production designers, and art directors to be certain that the furniture and backdrops used in scenes do not clash with the costumes. They meet with lighting designers to make sure that the lighting will not change the appearance of a costume's colors.

Depending on the production's budget, costume designers rent, purchase, or create costumes from scratch. They shop for clothing and accessories, fabrics, and sewing supplies. They also supervise assistants who sew or alter the costumes.

Education and Training

To become a costume designer, you need at least a high school education, but a college degree in costume design, fashion

DID YOU KNOW?

Where Costume Designers Work

- Fashion designers
- Film and television production companies
- Theatrical production companies

design, or fiber art is recommended. You should also have experience working in theater or film.

English and literature courses will help you read and understand scripts. History classes are helpful for researching historical costumes and time periods. Courses in sewing, art, designing, and draping are also necessary.

Earnings

Costume designers who work on Broadway (in New York City) or for other large stage productions are usually members of United Scenic Artists. This union sets the minimum fees that union costume designers can be paid for their work. According to the union, a costume designer for a Broadway show (dramatic) in 2009 earned anywhere from $7,332 (for creating costumes for a show with one to seven characters) to $16,463 (for a show with 36 or more characters). For off-Broadway shows, operas, and dance productions, salary is usually by costume count. For feature films and television, costume designers earn daily rates for an eight-hour day or a weekly rate for an unlimited number of hours. Costume designers working on major film or television productions earned union minimums of $2,776 for five days of work in 2009.

Most costume designers work for themselves and are paid per costume or show. Costume designers can charge between $90 and $500 per costume. Some costumes, such as those for figure skaters, can cost thousands of dollars.

Outlook

Little change is expected in the employment of costume designers. Designers face stiff competition. There are many more qualified costume designers than there are jobs. Jobs will be

FOR MORE INFO

This union represents costume designers in film and television. For information on the industry and to view costume sketches, visit its Web site.

Costume Designers Guild
11969 Ventura Boulevard, 1st Floor
Studio City, CA 91604-2630
818-752-2400
cdgia@costumedesignersguild.com
http://www.costumedesignersguild.com

For information on costume design, contact

Costume Society of America
390 Amwell Road, Suite 402
Hillsborough, NJ 08844-1247
800-272-9447
national.office@costumesocietyamerica.com
http://www.costumesocietyamerica.com

For industry information, contact

National Costumers Association
121 North Bosart Avenue
Indianapolis, IN 46201-3729

317-351-1940
office@costumers.org
http://www.costumers.org

This union represents costume designers and other design professionals. For information on apprenticeship programs and other resources on the career, contact

United Scenic Artists Local USA 829
29 West 38th Street, 15th Floor
New York, NY 10018-5504
212-581-0300
http://www.usa829.org

For information on opportunities in the performing arts and entertainment industry, contact

United States Institute for Theater Technology
315 South Crouse Avenue, Suite 200
Syracuse, NY 13210-1844
800-938-7488
http://www.usitt.org

hard to find in small and nonprofit theaters, due to smaller budgets and shows that require fewer costumes. There may be more costume design opportunities in cable television, which is growing rapidly and will continue to grow in the next decade. New York City and Hollywood are the hottest spots for costume designers.

Fashion Coordinators

What Fashion Coordinators Do

Fashion coordinators produce fashion shows and plan other ways to promote clothing companies and designers. They are employed by design firms, retail corporations, and apparel centers. Some work in the entertainment industry.

There are different types of fashion shows. *Vendor* or *designer shows* arrive at the fashion coordinator's office almost pre-packaged. The outfits are already accessorized and are boxed in the order the clothes should be shown. Commentary and backdrops also are supplied by the vendor or designer. To prepare for a vendor show, fashion coordinators only have to book models and set up a stage. Vendor shows typically take only a few days to produce.

Trend shows are put on by a retailer and are produced by the fashion coordinator and his or her staff. Coordinators put outfits and accessories together, plan the movements of the models and staging, and most importantly, decide on the theme or featured fashion trend. Trend shows are usually produced two or three times a year. They take a few weeks or a month to produce.

There are several steps to producing a show. First, a budget for the show is set. A budget is an overview of the amount of money that the coordinator can spend on each part of the show. Then models are selected. Coordinators often use *modeling agents* to find the best men, women, or children to show off the latest fashions. *Stylists* are hired to give the models and their clothes a finished look. *Hairdressers, makeup artists,*

EXPLORING

- Read books about fashion.
- Watch fashion shows on television or read up on shows in fashion magazines. Take note of the style and themes used for shows and how they relate to the fashions presented.
- Many high schools, colleges, and community centers put on fashion shows. See if you can volunteer. You may be able to help models with outfit changes, set up chairs, or pass out brochures.
- Produce a fashion show at your own school. You can use fellow classmates as models and clothing and accessories borrowed from family or friends.
- Talk to a fashion coordinator about his or her career.

and *dressers* prepare models before the show and during outfit changes. *Production workers* work to create the right music and lighting.

The fashion coordinator also has to promote the fashion show. They send invitations to the public and media. They prepare advertising as well as set up chairs and props and check on other last-minute details.

In addition to organizing shows, fashion coordinators promote their store's fashion lines through television, newspapers, magazine, and Internet exposure. Local television stations, newspapers, or fashion magazines sometimes borrow clothing from a store for a special shoot. The fashion coordinator pulls the appropriate clothing from the sales floor and delivers the chosen items to the TV station, newspaper, or magazine offices. The TV station or publication gives credit to the store in return for the use of the clothes.

DID YOU KNOW?

Style.com, the online home of the fashion magazine *Vogue,* has an entire section devoted to fashion shows. Visit http://www.style.com/fashionshows to see photos from recent shows, critics' picks for the most popular looks, and more.

Education and Training

High school classes that will prepare you for this career include family and consumer science, art, art history, illustration, photography, and business. Some high schools, such as the High School of Fashion Industries in New York City, offer fashion-related courses such as fashion design, illustration, fashion merchandising, and art and art history along with the more traditional academic classes. Check with schools in your area to see if any fashion-related classes are available.

A college education is not required to work as a fashion coordinator, but a bachelor's degree in fashion design and merchandising, marketing, or other business-related courses will give you an edge. Computer skills are also important.

Fashion Debuts

1700s: Blue jeans

1800s: Left- and right-footed shoes

1896: Buttoned-down collars

1916: Gym shoes

1926: Knee-length hemlines

1930: Designer logos on clothing

1940: Nylon stockings

1946: The bikini

1960s: Paper clothes

1978: Designer jeans

1995: Casual Fridays

2000s: Celebrity-designed clothing

Source: FactMonster.com

Earnings

There are no formal salary surveys available for this particular career. However, according to industry experts, most salaried coordinators should expect to earn from $40,000 to $60,000 annually. Coordinators working on a freelance basis can also earn as much, though they are paid only after a project is completed as opposed to every week or twice a month. Successful fashion coordinators who work

FOR MORE INFO

The AAFA represents "apparel, footwear and other sewn products companies, and their suppliers." Visit its Web site for information on endorsed college programs.

American Apparel & Footwear Association (AAFA)
http://www.apparelandfootwear.org

For industry information, contact
Fashion Group International
8 West 40th Street, 7th Floor
New York, NY 10018-2276
212-302-5511
http://newyork.fgi.org

To learn more about the programs and exhibitions offered at FIT, check out its Web site or contact

Fashion Institute of Technology (FIT)
227 West 27th Street
New York, NY 10001-5992
212-217-7999
http://www.fitnyc.edu

For a list of art and design schools, visit the following Web site
National Association of Schools of Art and Design
11250 Roger Bacon Drive, Suite 21
Reston, VA 20190-5248
703-437-0700
info@arts-accredit.org
http://nasad.arts-accredit.org

for larger corporations or well-known design houses can earn more than $100,000 a year.

Outlook

Employment in this career should be good for the next decade.

As fashion trends change, so will runway shows. Show themes reflect the taste of the consumer. Flashy styles translate to loud, heavily choreographed shows. Conservative styles may call for softer presentations. One style of show has no spoken commentary. Instead, messages in words and images are shown on backdrops. More recently, some companies have produced shows for both TV broadcast and the Internet. These new and varied types of shows should provide job opportunities for the creative fashion coordinator.

Fashion Designers

What Fashion Designers Do

Fashion designers design coats, dresses, suits, and other clothing. A small number of designers work in the fashion centers of the world: Paris, France; New York, United States; Milan, Italy; and London, United Kingdom. These high-profile designers create styles that set fashion trends for each season. Most designers, however, work for textile, apparel, and pattern manufacturers. Some work for fashion salons, high-fashion department stores, and specialty shops. A few design costumes for the theater and movies and television.

Designers first figure out what their customers want and need. Some designers make rough sketches and then draw flat pattern pieces on large sheets of paper. The patterns are laid on the fabric to provide cutting guidelines. Other designers use computer software to create designs. Computer-aided designing and computer-aided manufacturing allow for thousands of fashion styles and colors to be stored in a computer and accessed at the click of a mouse. This largely eliminates the long process of gathering fabrics and styling them into samples. Instead of using sketches or computer-aided design software, still other designers prefer to work directly with fabrics on a dressmaker dummy. They use inexpensive fabric, such as muslin, and pin or stitch the material directly on the dummy. Fabric pieces are then removed and used to make paper patterns.

Once the final pieces are cut and sewn, designers fit them on a model. This sample garment is shown to buyers, and

EXPLORING

- Read books about careers in fashion design.
- Practice your sewing skills. Start by using commercial patterns available at fabric stores. Frequent sewing will make you familiar with flat patterns and the various steps in clothing construction.
- Art and design courses will help you work on your sketching and drawing ability, and develop your color sense. The Fashion Institute of Technology in New York City offers fashion classes for middle school and high school students year-round. Visit http://www.fitnyc.edu/5915.asp for more information.
- Keep a sketchbook of fashion ideas. Collect fabric swatches and match them to the fashions you have drawn.
- Visit fabric stores and look at the materials available, including fabrics, buttons, threads, ribbons, and other notions.
- Attend fashion shows, visit art galleries, and observe clothing worn by fashion leaders.
- Talk to a fashion designer about his or her career.
- Visit the Museum at the Fashion Institute of Technology in New York City to learn more about fashion and fashion design. If you can't make it to New York, you can check out the museum's exhibitions online at http://fitnyc.edu/3662.asp.
- The Fashion Institute of Technology's Web site (http://www.fitnyc.edu/2127.asp) features photographs and videos of fashion design students and their work.

alterations are made as needed. In small shops, designers work on all phases of fashion production, from thinking up the original idea to sewing the completed garment. In larger companies, designers design and draw the original style, while the other work is left to *patternmakers*, *graders* (who draw the paper patterns in various sizes), and *sewers*.

Fashion designers who work for large firms that mass-produce clothing often create 50 to 150 designs for each season. They work on spring and summer designs during the fall and winter months, and work on fall and winter clothing during the spring and summer months.

There are many opportunities for fashion designers to specialize. The most common specialties are particular types of garments such as bridal wear, resort wear, or sportswear.

Some designers work for a few individual clients. In fact, many designers start out this way. As their reputation and

A fashion designer adjusts the belt on a patent leather coat he designed. (Kathy Willens, AP Photo)

Words to Learn

drape to hang a piece of fabric from a dressmaker dummy or a model

epaulette a shoulder ornament

fabric swatch a small sample of a piece of fabric

fashion the popular style of a culture that is demonstrated in clothing, hair, makeup, and accessories

haute couture the creation of exclusive fashions

inseam the interior seam on a pant leg

microfiber a synthetic fabric that is soft and ultrafine

season a time of the year when certain fashions, such as winter wear or summer wear, are made available to the public

number of clients grows, so does their business, until they are creating a full set of designs for each new season.

Designers must be creative, have the ability to draw, and work well with their hands. Math skills are important for converting a flat pattern into a shaped garment, sizing patterns, and measuring yardage. Computer skills are also necessary because most designers use computer programs to create and alter their designs before even touching a piece of fabric.

Education and Training

In high school, there are many courses that will prepare you for college training in fashion design. These include art, family and consumer science, math, and computer-aided design.

The best way to become a fashion designer is to complete a two- or three-year program in design from a fashion school. Some colleges offer a four-year degree in fine arts with a major in fashion design. Typical courses include mathematics, business, color theory, design, sketching, art history, fashion history, human anatomy, literature, pattern making, sewing and tailoring, clothing construction, and textiles. Many students

DID YOU KNOW?

There are four main rules of fashion design. They are as follows:

- Harmony: All parts of a fashion design should work together.
- Proportion: All parts of an outfit should relate to one another in size, length, and bulk.
- Emphasis: A garment should have one feature that attracts the eye.
- Balance: A garment should have equal interest in all directions from the main center of interest.

participate in internships that provide them with hands-on experience in the field.

Earnings

Fashion designers earned median annual salaries of $64,260 in 2009, according to the U.S. Department of Labor. New designers just starting out in the field earned less than $33,000. A few highly skilled and well-known designers in top firms have annual incomes of more than $130,000. Top fashion designers who have successful lines of clothing can earn bonuses that bring their annual incomes into the millions of dollars. Few designers are in this category.

Outlook

Little employment change is expected for fashion designers during the next decade. Good designers always will be needed, although not in great numbers. Increasing populations and growing personal incomes should increase the demand for fashion designers. Those who design clothing that is sold in department stores and retail chain stores will have the best job prospects.

FOR MORE INFO

The AAFA represents "apparel, footwear and other sewn products companies, and their suppliers." Visit its Web site for information on endorsed college programs.

American Apparel & Footwear Association (AAFA)
http://www.apparelandfootwear.org

For industry information, contact
Council of Fashion Designers of America
1412 Broadway, Suite 2006
New York, NY 10018-9250
http://www.cfda.com

Those interested in creating men's fashions should visit the CTDA Web site for business and training information.
Custom Tailors and Designers Association (CTDA)
42732 Ridgeway Drive
Broadlands, VA 20148-4558
888-248-2832
http://www.ctda.com

Fashion Group International is a non-profit association of 5,000 professionals in the fashion, apparel, accessories, beauty, and home industries. Visit its Web site for information about the fashion industry.
Fashion Group International Inc.
8 West 40th Street, 7th Floor
New York, NY 10018-2276
212-302-5511
http://newyork.fgi.org

To learn more about the programs and exhibitions offered at FIT, check out its Web site or contact
Fashion Institute of Technology
227 West 27th Street
New York, NY 10001-5992
212-217-7999
http://www.fitnyc.edu

For industry information, contact
International Association of Clothing Designers & Executives
835 Northwest 36th Terrace
Oklahoma City, OK 73118-7104
405-602-8037
http://www.iacde.net

For a listing of accredited design schools and information on choosing the best program, contact
National Association of Schools of Art and Design
11250 Roger Bacon Drive, Suite 21
Reston, VA 20190-5248
703-437-0700
info@arts-accredit.org
http://nasad.arts-accredit.org

For information on careers in the sewn products industry, including fashion design, contact
Career Threads.com
http://www.careerthreads.com

For subscription information, visit the following magazine's Web site:
Women's Wear Daily
http://www.wwd.com

Fashion Illustrators

What Fashion Illustrators Do

Fashion illustrators create drawings, or illustrations, that appear in print and electronic formats. Illustrations are used to advertise new fashions, promote models, and popularize certain designers.

Some illustrators provide artwork to accompany editorial pieces in magazines such as *Glamour, Redbook,* and *Seventeen* and newspapers such as *Women's Wear Daily.* Catalog companies also hire illustrators to provide the artwork that sells their merchandise through print or online publications.

Fashion illustrators work with fashion designers, editors, and models. They make sketches from designers' notes or they may sketch live models during runway shows or other fashion presentations. They use pencils, pen and ink, charcoal, paint, airbrush, or a combination of media to create their work. Today, many fashion illustrators use computer-aided drawing programs to create illustrations.

Fashion illustrators should have a love of fashion and have artistic skill. In addition to working with pens and paper, fashion illustrators also need to be able to work with computer programs designed to manipulate their artwork. They should also have good business sense (especially if they work as freelancers) to be able to sell their work to employers, bill clients promptly and appropriately, and keep records of their work organized. Illustrators who work for magazines or newspapers may work long hours to meet publication deadlines. Other important traits include an eye for detail and good communication skills.

EXPLORING

- Read books about fashion illustration.
- Visit http://fashionbook.com to view portfolios of illustrators and other fashion professionals.
- Join your school's yearbook, newspaper, or literary magazine. These publications often include student illustrations along with text.
- Apply for a part-time job at an art supply or retail clothing store.
- Read fashion magazines and visit Web sites that include fashion sketches to see what others are doing and to learn about the latest fashion trends and models.
- The best way to see if you have what it takes to become a fashion illustrator is to start drawing. Use the following Web site to help you practice drawing basic modeling figures and read tips about using other materials such as glue, pens, and mounting boards: Fashion Drawing Tutorial Tips (http://www.fashion-era.com/drawing_fashion.htm).
- Talk to a fashion illustrator about his or her career.

Education and Training

There are a number of classes you can take in high school to help you prepare for this work. Naturally, take as many studio art classes, such as drawing and painting, as you can. Computer classes that teach you about computer-aided design will also be useful. Business and math classes will give you skills you will need to keep track of your accounts and run your own business. Take English or communication classes to develop your communication skills.

After high school, consider enrolling in a fashion illustration program at an art school, university, community college, or

DID YOU KNOW?

Where Fashion Illustrators Work

- Book publishers
- Design or advertising firms
- Fashion firms (called houses)
- Fashion Web sites
- Large retailers
- Magazines
- Newspapers
- Self-employment

DID YOU KNOW?

Illustration featured prominently in the ancient civilizations of Mesopotamia, Egypt, and later Greek and Roman civilizations. Drawings of figures conveying power or ideas have also been found among ancient Assyrian, Babylonian, Egyptian, and Chinese societies. Modern illustration began during the Renaissance of the 15th and 16th centuries, with the work of Leonardo da Vinci, Andreas Vesalius, and Michelangelo Buonarotti.

adult education center. A college degree is not necessary to become a fashion illustrator, but it will give you the chance to build a portfolio. A portfolio is a collection of an artist's best sketches to show to prospective clients and employers.

Earnings

The U.S. Department of Labor reports that salaried fine artists, including illustrators, had median yearly incomes of approximately $44,160 in 2009. Earnings ranged from less than $20,000 to more than $86,000. Their earning potential depends on where their work is published. A large fashion magazine is able to pay more for an illustration than a small publisher. Illustrators that build a strong portfolio of published work and work for more well-known clients can make hundreds of thousands of dollars a year.

Outlook

Employment for visual artists, including illustrators, is expected to be good during the next decade. But since many people want to become fashion illustrators, it will be hard to land a job. The employment of illustrators specifically working in fashion will depend on the success of magazines, newspapers, advertising firms, and fashion houses. The outlook for these employers currently looks fair. Illustrators who are creative and persistent in finding job leads will be the most successful.

FOR MORE INFO

For information on union membership, contact

Graphic Artists Guild
32 Broadway, Suite 1114
New York, NY 10004-1612
212-791-3400
http://www.graphicartistsguild.org

For information on illustration education and careers, contact

Society of Illustrators
128 East 63rd Street
New York, NY 10065-7303
212-838-2560
info@societyillustrators.org
http://www.societyillustrators.org

Fashion Models

What Fashion Models Do

Many people know about the beautiful supermodels who wear expensive clothing and have their pictures taken all over the world. But *fashion models* of all ages, shapes and sizes, and backgrounds work in this field. They act in television commercials, pose for photographers and artists, appear in fashion shows, and help sell products in stores and at conventions.

Fashion models work in a variety of settings, exhibiting clothes and accessories (hats, shoes, etc.). Although the work may appear to be fun and exciting, it is demanding and difficult. Many fashion models pose for photographs or illustrations used in advertising brochures and sales catalogs. One photograph may be taken in a studio under hot lights with the model wearing a heavy fur coat. Another may be taken outdoors in cold weather with the model wearing only a bathing suit. One job may last an hour, while another may require an entire day. Fashion models may travel all over the United States and to foreign countries to be photographed in exotic or unusual settings.

In large stores, fashion models are employed to help sell various products. The store may have a regularly scheduled fashion show during the lunch hour. These models walk down a runway modeling the newest clothing designs for consumers and store buyers. At other times, the models may walk throughout the store showing clothing or other apparel and talking with customers about the garments.

There are significant differences in the requirements necessary for each type of model. The major requirement for the

EXPLORING

- Visit http://models.com to read about fashions, models, and agencies.
- Read books about modeling.
- If you are interested in a modeling career, gather information from a variety of sources, including agencies, modeling schools, books, and articles. Little information is available to help you in deciding which agency to approach other than checking with your local branch of the Better Business Bureau or chamber of commerce and talking with experienced models.
- Talk to a fashion model about his or her career. Ask the following questions: What made you want to become a model?, What do you like most and least about your job?, What advice would you give to someone interested in the career?
- Participate in community or school fashion shows as a model.

fashion model is, of course, physical appearance. Although most people think of all models as being young and slender, that is not necessarily the case. No set standard exists for a model's physical description because many different body types are needed.

Specialty models must have particular features that are photogenic (or look good in photographs or videos) that will help sell specific products. These features include hands, feet, legs, hair, lips, or ears.

Models should be physically attractive but do not need to be extremely beautiful or handsome. They must have a neat appearance and a pleasant personality. They must be able to

A model shows a designer's creation during a fashion show. (Kirsty Wigglesworth, AP Photo)

work under stressful conditions. The ability to stay in good condition (getting the proper amount of sleep, keeping a strict diet, and exercising) also is important. Finally, the ability to handle rejection is critical because models often compete at auditions with many other qualified candidates for only one or two jobs.

Education and Training

There are no standard educational requirements for models. Most employers of photographic models prefer at least a high school education. Courses such as sewing, art, family and consumer science, and photography are helpful. Although models come in all shapes and sizes, it won't hurt to stay in good shape by participating in physical education classes.

There is no best way to become a model. Physical appearance and the ability to present clothing or products in an interesting manner are more important than educational background. Many models attend modeling schools, where they learn the skills and techniques of the business. Others take courses in dancing or physical fitness to improve their health and learn to move more gracefully.

DID YOU KNOW?

Where Fashion Models Work

- Apparel firms
- Fashion design houses
- Fashion model agencies
- Retail stores
- Self-employment

Earnings

Earnings for models vary according to their experience and depend on the number, length, and type of assignments received. Fashion models who worked full time earned $27,330 a year in 2009, according to the U.S. Department of Labor. Annual salaries ranged from less than $17,000 to more than $55,000. Wages are higher for photographic models working in large cities such as New York, Los Angeles, or Chicago and for models who are in great demand. Female models usually make more money than male models. Top photographic models signed to exclusive contracts with cosmetic firms may earn $1 million or more per year. Almost all models work with agents and pay 10 to 15 percent of their earnings in return for an agent's services.

Outlook

Employment is expected to be good for models, but job competition will be fierce because this career is attractive to so many

Fame & Fortune: Tyra Banks

It's hard to believe the supermodel and television personality Tyra Banks ever felt unhappy and insecure about her looks. But as young girl, she never felt like she fit in. A sudden growth spurt at age 11 left her much taller than her classmates. She was also extremely skinny. Even as she grew into her height during her teens, Banks still had little luck with Los Angeles area modeling agencies. They simply felt, according to a story about Banks in *People* magazine, that Tyra was "too ethnic." Not the case in Paris, France.

Just weeks before Banks was about to start college, her unique look caught the attention of a French modeling scout who quickly signed Tyra to work high fashion shows in Paris. The self-described "beanpole freak" no longer had to worry about standing out from the norm. Top designers were so entranced with Banks she was booked for an unprecedented 25 shows her first full week in Paris!

Banks went on to work extensively—for runway and print—with many of the world's top designers and fashion manufacturers including Chanel, Dolce & Gabbana, CoverGirl, Victoria's Secret, and Swatch. Her grace and confidence on the catwalk, plus her strong work ethic and pleasant attitude, made her a favorite among many designers and photographers.

Banks was also the first African American model to land on the covers of *GQ* magazine and the *Sports Illustrated Swimsuit Issue*—appearing in both in the same year. In 1997, she was the cover choice for the *Victoria's Secret* catalog, as well as winning VH1's Supermodel of the Year award.

Not satisfied with her success as a model, Banks decided to branch out into other fields. She wrote the book *Tyra's Beauty: Inside and Out* to help young women make the most of their true features and natural beauty. Tyra also began her move into the entertainment industry with appearances in numerous films and television shows, and two R&B music singles.

Officially retired as a model since 2005, Banks now focuses her energy on creating a media empire. She is currently the host and executive producer of the fashion reality shows *America's Next Top Model* and *Stylista,* and is the host of the syndicated talk show *The Tyra Banks Show.* Banks has certainly proven herself to be a successful mix of beauty and brains.

Sources: *People,* Tyra.com

people. The number of fashion models seeking jobs is far greater than the number of openings. Part-time work is easier to find than full-time work. Most openings will occur as models quit or retire to pursue other jobs or interests. More jobs are expected to be available for male models in the future.

FOR MORE INFO

For information on modeling careers and annual conventions, visit this Web site.
International Modeling and Talent Association
http://www.imta.com

Fashion Models' Agents

What Fashion Models' Agents Do

Fashion models' agents are the link joining the talent (the model) with an employer (clients who have jobs for models). Agents match models to jobs according to a particular "look" the client desires.

An agent's job may begin when a client contacts the agency with a possible job assignment. The client, for example, a retail store, usually will have a specific look in mind for the model. The look may include such aspects as the model's hair color, age group, body type, or ethnicity. Once the look has been decided, the agent refers to his or her "comp board." This list displays pictures and details about the models represented by the agency.

The agent then sends a group of models that fit the desired look to the client for an audition. If the model is chosen for the job, then he or she is booked, or given the assignment.

In addition to finding models jobs, agents also arrange for the model's transportation if the assign-

EXPLORING

- Read books and magazines about the fashion industry.
- Hone your selling abilities by getting a part-time or seasonal job at a retail store. Whether you are selling an article of clothing or a model's talent, what's important is your ability to market and sell a product.
- Attend a model convention or search. Elite Model Management, for example, conducts an annual "Look of the Year" contest held in several cities nationwide. You will be able to observe the process potential models go through as well as see agents at work.
- Talk to an agent about his or her career.

ment is out of town. They also type up call sheets. A call sheet is a notice containing all the important information regarding the modeling assignment, such as whether it is a photo shoot, fashion show, or product demonstration. Location and time are listed on the call sheet, as well as how the model is expected to look—full makeup and styled hair or clean face and hair.

Tips for Success

To be a successful fashion models' agent, you should

- be an expert on the fashion industry
- be able to recognize and promote talent
- be able to work well with others— especially models who sometimes have big egos
- enjoy traveling
- be highly organized
- have a confident personality

While agents maintain good working relationships with current clients, they also look for new clients and more assignment possibilities. In addition, agents constantly search for new models. Modeling shows and conventions are held through the year all over the United States and in other countries. Agents attend these shows to scout for models, interview them, and perhaps offer them modeling contracts.

Education and Training

Take classes such as family and consumer science and art in high school. Business and math classes will help you later when working with modeling contracts and negotiating salaries. English and speech classes will help you develop your communication skills. If your high school offers any sales and marketing courses, be sure to take those. Some high schools offer curriculum targeted to fashion, which may include classes in design, illustration, and sewing. Sign up for these if they're available.

A high school diploma is necessary for work as a fashion model agent. While a college degree is helpful, you don't necessarily need one to get ahead in this industry. Much of the

Fashion Model Agencies on the Web

- **Elite Model Management Corporation**
  http://www.elitemodel.com
- **Ford Models**
  http://www.fordmodels.com
- **Marilyn Agency**
  http://www.marilynagency.com
- **ModelScouts**
  http://www.modelscouts.com
- **Wilhelmina Models**
  http://www.wilhelmina.com

training is obtained while on the job.

Earnings

Salaries for fashion models' agents vary depending on such factors as the agent's experience, the size and location of their agency, and the models they represent. Median annual salaries for agents and business managers of artists, performers, and athletes were $61,890 in 2009, according to the U.S. Department of Labor. New agents earned less than $26,000. Agents at the top of the industry may make $166,000 or more.

Some agents are paid on commission. This means they earn a percentage of the fees generated by model/client bookings. Commission rates normally range from 10 to 15 percent of model booking totals. For example, if a model receives $1,000 for a photo shoot, an agent with a commission rate of 10 percent would receive $100 as his or her fee.

Outlook

The fashion industry is an exciting field, and many people want to work in it. This makes it tough to land a job as an agent. Despite this, there will continue to be a need for skilled agents. Since most clients prefer to work with modeling agencies, very few models succeed without the support of an agency. New York City will continue to be the hub of modeling in the United

FOR MORE INFO

For industry information, contact
Fashion Group International Inc.
8 West 40th Street, 7th Floor
New York, NY 10018-2276
212-302-5511
http://newyork.fgi.org

For information about this school, admissions requirements, and exhibits at The Museum at FIT, contact
Fashion Institute of Technology (FIT)
227 West 27th Street
New York, NY 10001-5992
212-217-7999
http://www.fitnyc.edu

For information about the modeling industry and a listing of modeling agencies in the United States and in other countries, visit the following Web site:
The Insider's Guide to Supermodels and Modeling
http://www.supermodelguide.com

To read about fashions, models, and agencies, check out this Web site.
Models.com
http://models.com

States. Many large agencies will stay headquartered there. Some models' agents may find more jobs by representing actors and actresses. Other agents represent models who are hired for specific body parts. The most popular areas of specialization include legs, feet, and hands.

Fashion Photographers

What Fashion Photographers Do

Fashion photographers shoot pictures of the exciting world of fashion. They take and develop pictures of people, places, and objects while using a variety of cameras and photographic equipment. Photographs are used to promote fashions, models, and designers.

The advertising industry is the largest employer of fashion photographers. These artists create the pictures that sell clothing, cosmetics, shoes, accessories, and beauty products. Large retailers that publish catalogs of their goods also hire fashion illustrators to shoot images of models, clothing, shoes, and other merchandise. Some photographers work on staff or as freelancers for fashion magazines or newspapers.

Fashion photographers work on a team with designers, editors, illustrators, models, hair stylists, photo stylists, and makeup artists. They take photographs in a studio or on location, indoors and outdoors. Photographers use cameras, film, filters, lenses, lighting equipment, props, and sets. Their main goal is to satisfy the client's requirements. Some photographers become known for their unique styles and artistic vision and become sought after to work on many fashion shoots.

In addition to being skilled at photography, fashion photographers should also be able to use new technologies such as digital cameras and computer programs designed to store and edit images.

Photographers may work as freelancers, handling all the business aspects that go along with being self-employed. Such

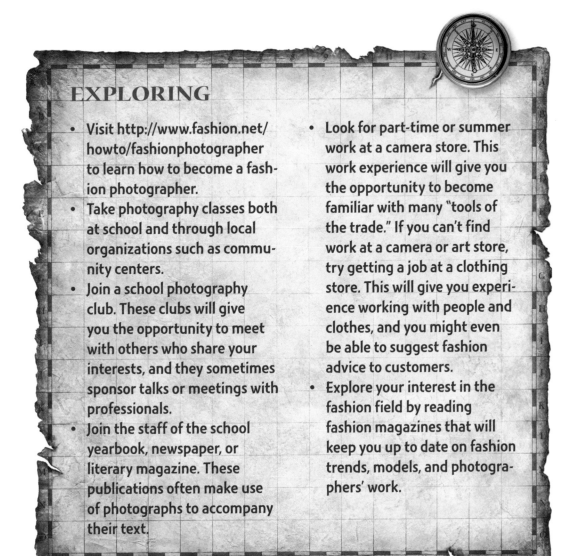

EXPLORING

- Visit http://www.fashion.net/howto/fashionphotographer to learn how to become a fashion photographer.
- Take photography classes both at school and through local organizations such as community centers.
- Join a school photography club. These clubs will give you the opportunity to meet with others who share your interests, and they sometimes sponsor talks or meetings with professionals.
- Join the staff of the school yearbook, newspaper, or literary magazine. These publications often make use of photographs to accompany their text.
- Look for part-time or summer work at a camera store. This work experience will give you the opportunity to become familiar with many "tools of the trade." If you can't find work at a camera or art store, try getting a job at a clothing store. This will give you experience working with people and clothes, and you might even be able to suggest fashion advice to customers.
- Explore your interest in the fashion field by reading fashion magazines that will keep you up to date on fashion trends, models, and photographers' work.

duties include keeping track of expenses, billing clients, and keeping their businesses going by lining up new jobs for when a current project ends.

Because the fashion world is extremely competitive and fast-paced, photographers tend to work long hours under the pressure of deadlines and demanding personalities.

Supermodel Elle Macpherson poses for photographers outside a retail store. (Matt Dunham, AP Photo)

Education and Training

In high school, take as many art classes as possible—especially photography courses. Try to sign up for computer classes that teach you how to use photo-editing software such as Adobe Photoshop. If you plan to run your own business, be sure to take business, math, and accounting classes. English and communication classes will help you to develop your communication skills. It is important to be able to communicate effectively with clients and models.

If you want to become a fashion photographer, you have many training options. You may decide to study fashion design and work on your photography skills on the side. Or you could focus your studies on photography but also take some classes in fashion. In addition, there are academic programs in fashion photography at many colleges and universities. Many community and junior colleges offer associate's degrees in photography or commercial art. While a college degree is not required, these programs will help you develop your skills, meet contacts in the fashion or photography industries and, most importantly, build up your portfolio. A portfolio is a collection of your best fashion pictures that show employers the scope of your talent. A portfolio is almost always required when looking for a job in fashion photography.

Earnings

According to the U.S. Department of Labor, the median annual pay for salaried photographers was approximately $29,770 in 2009. The lowest paid 10 percent made less than $18,000, while the highest paid 10 percent made more than $62,000 per year.

Fashion photographers who own their own businesses and work on a freelance basis are typically paid by the job. The pay for these jobs may be based on such factors as the photographer's reputation, the prestige of the client (for example, a fashion magazine with an international readership will pay more for photos than a local newspaper doing a Sunday fashion spread), and the difficulty of the work. For some of this work, photographers may make $250 to $300 per job. They may also get

Tips for Success

To be a successful fashion photographer, you should

- have a strong interest in the fashion industry
- have artistic ability
- be skilled at using digital cameras, computer software programs, and related technology
- have an eye for detail
- be able to work under deadline pressure
- be willing to work long hours to meet deadlines and to achieve your artistic goals
- have good business skills if you own your own business
- have confidence in your abilities and artistic vision

credit lines (their name accompanying the photo) and receive travel expenses. As they gain experience, photographers can make $2,000 per job or more. Freelance photographers who have national or international reputations can make $100,000 or more per year.

Outlook

Employment for photographers in general is expected to be good during the next decade. The employment outlook for fashion photographers is not as strong since many people want to become fashion photographers. Despite the challenge of landing a job, magazines, newspapers, advertising firms, and fashion houses will always need trained photographers to capture the latest styles. Employment opportunities will also be found in new media outlets such as e-zines and retail Web sites.

Profile: Bruce Weber (1946–   )

Bruce Weber is a well-known American fashion photographer. He is best known for his black and white photographs. Today, his work is sought after by some of the biggest fashion companies (known as fashion houses), including Abercrombie & Fitch, Gianni Versace, Ralph Lauren, and Pirelli.

Weber got his start in fashion photography with spreads appearing in *GQ* magazine in the 1970s, as well as the catalog for the retailing giant, Bloomingdale's. He gained the public's attention in the late 1980s with his work for fashion designer Calvin Klein. During this time, Weber took some of his most well-known photographs.

Weber has also photographed musicians such as Chris Isaak, Jackson Browne, and Harry Connick, Jr. In the 1990s, Bruce began to direct music videos and films. In recent years, he has taken photographs of actors, including Taylor Lautner and Robert Pattinson of *Twilight* fame. Visit Bruceweber.com to learn more about his career and to see samples of his work.

Sources: Bruceweber.com, Buzzle.com

FOR MORE INFO

For information on photography careers, contact
Professional Photographers of America
229 Peachtree Street, NE, Suite 2200
Atlanta, GA 30303-1608
800-786-6277
csc@ppa.com
http://www.ppa.com

This Web site allows you to browse through galleries of hundreds of established fashion photographers.
FashionBook.com
http://www.fashionbook.com/photographers

However, the *Occupational Outlook Handbook* notes that the growing popularity of digital cameras and computer programs can allow consumers and businesses to produce and access photographic images on their own. Despite this improved technology, the specialized skills of the trained photographer should still find demand in the fashion world.

Fashion Public Relations Specialists

EXPLORING

- Read books about fashion and public relations.
- Develop your interpersonal skills by seeking out opportunities to work with other people.
- Join your school newspaper or yearbook staff to work on your writing and reporting skills.
- A job in clothing retail will give you fashion experience and help you to understand some of the principles of product presentation.
- Volunteering to help with a political campaign can expose you to how PR specialists use persuasive speaking and writing tactics and how they deal with the media.
- Talk to a public relations specialist about his or her career.

What Fashion Public Relations Specialists Do

Fashion public relations specialists help fashion houses, retailers, and other organizations that sell fashion items present a good image to the public. Fashion public relations (PR) specialists include executives, writers, artists, and researchers. These specialists work together to provide information to the public and media about a company, its accomplishments, and goals for the future. Their work helps to promote the company's reputation in hopes of selling more clothing, shoes, jewelry, or other merchandise. Fashion PR specialists are also known as *fashion publicists.*

Fashion PR specialists spend much of their time writing. They write reports, news releases, booklets, speeches, and text (called copy) for radio and television ads. PR specialists also edit employee publications, newsletters, and reports to shareholders. Many also write and edit copy that appears on company Web sites. All of this writing and editing has one goal: to offer the public positive information about a fashion designer, house, or company.

Contact with the media is another important part of fashion PR specialists' jobs. They promote their company through radio, television, newspapers, magazines, and Web sites (including social network sites such as Facebook). They also use special events to get their messages across. Press parties, fashion runway shows, and open houses help to establish good feelings and a positive image between the company and the media, which reports the events to the public.

Most large retailers and fashion houses have their own public relations departments and hire their own workers. Other companies hire outside firms whose workers provide PR services to one or more companies. In either case, these workers must be specialists in not only PR, but in fashion trends as well. To keep up with the latest styles, PR workers do research or conduct public opinion polls. Polls ask random people questions about their interests. For example, a PR specialist might ask people of different ages what brands of clothing they buy. This research helps the industry analyze which fashions are popular among different age groups. From this information, they can develop a PR plan for their company and put it into action.

Education and Training

Most public relations specialists are college graduates, so it is important to take college preparatory courses, especially English, speech, humanities, and languages in high school. Writing is an important part of public relations, so you should build your writing skills, perhaps by working on school publications.

In college, pursue a degree in public relations, English, communications, journalism, or business. A graduate degree is often required for top positions. Many students participate in internships to gain hands-on experience in the field. Some

Visit The Museum of Public Relations

In late 1997, Spector & Associates debuted the Museum of Public Relations on the Web. This online museum is meant to provide a history and examples of successful public relations programs for industry, education, and government, using photographs and stories. Read about such public relations trendsetters as Edward L. Bernays, Moss Kendrix, Carl R. Byoir, Arthur W. Page, and Chester Burger. For more information, visit http://www.prmuseum.com.

companies have training programs for newly hired PR specialists. In other companies, new employees work closely under the supervision of more experienced specialists. They read and file newspaper and magazine articles, perform research, and learn to write press releases.

Earnings

Public relations specialists, especially those employed by large fashion houses and companies, can earn high salaries. Earnings will vary, however, depending on the individual's experience, education, and job duties within the company.

The U.S. Department of Labor reports that public relations specialists had median annual earnings of $51,960 in 2009. Those just starting out in the field earned less than $31,000. Very experienced PR specialists made more than $96,000. Specialists with many years of experience and managerial duties can earn $125,000 or more. These executives may serve as a company vice president or in other managerial positions.

Outlook

Employment growth for PR professionals in all industries is expected to be very good during the next decade. Job opportunities in the fashion industry will not be as strong because fewer people work in this specialty and many people want to enter the field. Competition is strong for beginning jobs. People with both education and experience will have an advantage. For fashion PR jobs, individuals with both PR skills and previous experience in fashion retail should have an advantage.

Most large fashion employers have some sort of public relations resource, either through their own staff or through the use of an outside PR company. Even small fashion businesses will continue to need help communicating their image to the public, so PR workers should stay in demand in coming years.

Profile: Eleanor Lambert (1903–2003), Fashion PR Specialist

Eleanor Lambert worked long in the fashion industry to promote American designers, such as Bill Blass, Oscar de la Renta, Calvin Klein, and Halston, during a time when French designers were all that mattered in the fashion world. As early as the 1920s, Lambert challenged the prevailing view that the source of all fashion was Paris. In 1943, to prove her point, she organized fashion shows so that the press could preview American designer collections all in one venue. These shows, revolutionary in their scope and inclusion, became the precursor to today's New York Fashion Week.

Source: *Chicago Sun-Times*

FOR MORE INFO

For career information and PR news, contact
Council of Public Relations Firms
317 Madison Avenue, Suite 2320
New York, NY 10017-5205
877-773-4767
http://www.prfirms.org

For industry information, contact
International Association of Business Communicators
601 Montgomery Street, Suite 1900
San Francisco, CA 94111-2623

415-544-4700
http://www.iabc.com

For statistics, salary surveys, and other information about the profession, contact
Public Relations Society of America
33 Maiden Lane, 11th Floor
New York, NY 10038-5150
212-460-1400
http://www.prsa.org

Fashion Writers and Editors

What Fashion Writers and Editors Do

Fashion writers express their ideas about fashion in words for books, magazines, newspapers, advertisements, radio, television, and the Internet. These writing jobs require a combination of creativity and hard work. Fashion writers are also known as *fashion reporters, correspondents,* and *authors.*

Most fashion writers work for fashion magazines. These writers report on fashion news, interview top designers, and write feature articles on the latest styles for a season (a time of the year when certain fashions are introduced to the public). Fashion writers also work for newspapers that have fashion sections (often a part of a larger arts-and-entertainment department), Web sites, or other media outlets. Other fashion writers work for book publishers.

Good fashion writers gather as much information as possible

EXPLORING

- To improve your writing skills, read, read, read! Read all kinds of writing—not just fashion articles. Fiction, nonfiction, poetry, and essays will introduce you to many different forms of writing.
- Work as a reporter, writer, or editor on school newspapers, yearbooks, and literary magazines.
- Start a journal and write in it every day. Try not to worry about grammar, punctuation, and spelling. The important thing is to express yourself freely.
- Write articles about the latest fashion trends, a fashion show that is held at your school or in your community, or other fashion-related topics.
- Talk to fashion writers and editors about their careers.

about the subject and then carefully check the accuracy of their sources. This can involve extensive library research, interviews, and long hours of observation and personal experience. Writers usually keep notes from which they prepare an outline or summary. They use this outline to write a first draft and then rewrite sections of their material, always searching for the best way to express their ideas. Generally, their writing will be reviewed, corrected, and revised many times before a final copy is ready for publication.

Fashion editors work with fashion writers on the staffs of newspapers, magazines, publishing houses, radio or television stations, and corporations of all kinds. Their main job is to make sure that text provided by fashion writers is suitable in content, format, and style for the intended audiences. For example, a fashion editor working for a newspaper would make sure that articles are timely and can be understood and enjoyed by the newspaper's average reader—not just people in the fashion industry.

Editors must make sure that all text is well written, factually correct (sometimes this job is done by a *researcher* or *fact checker*), and grammatically correct. Other editors, including *managing editors, editors-in-chief,* and *editorial directors,* have managerial responsibilities and work with heads of other departments, such as marketing, sales, and production.

Education and Training

In high school, take English, journalism, and communications courses. To gain a better understanding of fashion and design, take classes in family and consumer science, including sewing and design, if they are available. The fashion industry is located throughout the world, so taking a foreign language, such as French or Italian, will also be helpful. Other useful courses include computer science and typing.

Vogue *editor Anna Wintour (left) and designer Tory Burch discuss Burch's new designs during a Fashion Week event.* (Richard Drew, AP Photo)

A college education is usually necessary if you want to become a writer or editor. You should also know how to use a computer for word processing and be able to handle the pressure of deadlines. Employers prefer to hire people who have a communications, English, or journalism degree. Fashion writers and editors must know a lot about their subject, so classes in fashion design and marketing are also useful. Some writers and editors may have a college degree in fashion or a

DID YOU KNOW?

Good writing takes practice. Fashion writers and editors need to be creative and unique—which takes practice. To keep your own creative juices flowing, try these critical thinking and writing exercises.

- Pick one of your favorite books to review. What is it about the book that you like? The plot? The author's writing style? The characters?
- Find a fashion article in a newspaper or magazine. Describe what the article is about. Does the article include photographs? If so, what do they add to the piece? If the fashion writer states opinions about new fashion styles, do you agree or disagree? Why? Would you write the article differently? If so, how?
- Look at some of the latest fashions in magazines and on the Internet. Write an article that describes the styles and what you think about each outfit.

related field in addition to a degree in English, journalism, or communications.

Earnings

Beginning fashion writers earn salaries that range from $20,000 to $26,000 per year. Most writers earned between $38,000 and $75,000 a year in 2009, according to the U.S. Department of Labor (DOL). Best-selling authors can earn more than $100,000 per year, but they are few in number.

The salaries of fashion editors are roughly comparable to those of other editors. Median annual earnings for all editors were $50,800 in 2009, according to the DOL. Salaries ranged from less than $28,000 to $97,000 or more. Beginning salaries of $20,000 or less are still common in many areas.

Outlook

Little change is expected in the employment of editors during the next decade, while employment for writers is expected to be

Fame & Fortune: Anna Wintour

Anna Wintour is not only the editor in chief of the American edition of *Vogue*. She is also a fashion industry leader.

Wintour began her career in fashion at an early age. She began working at a fashionable London boutique when she was only 15 years old. She honed her fashion journalism skills working for several noted magazines such as *Harper's & Queen, Savvy,* and *New York.* When she finally landed her coveted position at *Vogue,* Wintour was already known in the fashion industry as a strong-willed and hard-working woman, with a keen fashion sense.

At *Vogue,* Wintour made several key changes that radically altered the scope of the magazine. She often mixed inexpensive clothing with high-end fashion pieces. Her first *Vogue* cover featured a young model wearing denim jeans (a first for the magazine) paired with a $10,000 bejeweled haute couture (high, or exclusive, fashion) T-shirt. Wintour also favored full body shots with natural lighting. She made sure to give credit to photographers, makeup artists, and hairstylists in the magazine.

Another one of Wintour's key changes was to feature celebrities on the front cover, which led to the end of the supermodel era. She found that the magazine sold better whenever a popular actress or entertainer was on the cover. Anna also used her many friends and contacts to secure unique settings for fashion shows and photo shoots. Many new designers, photographers, models, and artists owe their careers to Wintour, as she often promoted their talent within the magazine. Wintour also made changes in the editorial content of the magazine by featuring many stories on travel, business, and politics. She wanted to reach out to the new American woman—one who was interested in fashion, but also the world outside of fashion.

Wintour also played a key role in starting up three new magazines—*Teen Vogue, Vogue Living,* and *Men's Vogue. Teen Vogue* has been very successful.

Wintour is a fixture at many top fashions shows throughout the world—front row, of course—wearing her signature short bob hairstyle and large sunglasses. Always dressed sharply and current, Wintour is known for setting fashion trends.

However, fashion is not her only passion. Wintour is known for her many charity projects, many of which help the fashion industry and the city of New York.

Sources: Biography.com, *Vogue*

FOR MORE INFO

This organization of book publishers offers an extensive Web site for people interested in learning more about the book business.

Association of American Publishers
71 Fifth Avenue, 2nd Floor
New York, NY 10003-3004
212-255-0200
http://www.publishers.org

This organization is a good source of information about the magazine industry.

Association of Magazine Media
810 Seventh Avenue, 24th Floor
New York, NY 10019-5873
212-872-3700
mpa@magazine.org
http://www.magazine.org

For industry information, contact
Fashion Group International Inc.
8 West 40th Street, 7th Floor
New York, NY 10018-2276
212-302-5511
http://newyork.fgi.org

For information on educational programs in fashion, contact
National Association of Schools of Art and Design
11250 Roger Bacon Drive, Suite 21
Reston, VA 20190-5248
703-437-0700
info@arts-accredit.org
http://nasad.arts-accredit.org

good. Jobs should be available at newspapers, magazines, book publishers, advertising agencies, businesses, Web sites, and nonprofit organizations. The best opportunities for employment should be in small newspapers, radio stations, and television stations. In these organizations, pay is low even by the standards of the publishing business.

Many people want to become fashion writers and editors. This makes it difficult to land a job in the field—especially because there are only a small number of positions available. Those with previous experience and specialized education in fashion and reporting will have the best chances of finding jobs.

Knit Goods Industry Workers

What Knit Goods Industry Workers Do

Knit goods industry workers operate and repair the machines that knit various products, such as sweaters, socks, hats, sweatshirts, undergarments, lace, and other apparel. *Designers* create patterns and then choose the colors and yarn to make them. *Production managers* supervise the making of garments and keep track of costs and other important work records. *Knitters* and other workers actually make the finished product.

Although some workers still knit fabrics by hand, most commercial knitting is done by machine. Machines make knitted fabrics in much the same way it is done by hand: by forming loops of yarn with needles and then stitching them together with other loops. Machines, however, can knit thousands of stitches per second. This allows many more items to be made in a fraction of the time.

EXPLORING

- Talk to your parents or a teacher about touring a knitting mill. If you do not live near one, consider contacting a knit goods industry worker who is located elsewhere and conduct an information interview over the phone.
- To learn about machine repair, consider joining a club that focuses on mechanics.
- Take up knitting, needlepoint, or sewing to learn about the yarns, needles, machines, and other equipment knit goods industry workers use.
- Read books about knitting and related topics.

DID YOU KNOW?

Where Knit Goods Industry Professionals Work

- Apparel knitting mills
- Fabric mills
- Fiber, yarn, and thread mills
- Textile furnishings mills
- Other textile product mills

Many knitters and other workers are needed to operate these high-speed machines. Knitters put spools of yarn onto each machine and fasten the yarn to the machine's needles. While the machine is in operation, knitters replace spools of yarn as needed. They watch for any problems, such as yarn or needles breaking. Knitters are also usually responsible for keeping the machines in good working order. They grease the needles so that they run smoothly and keep the rest of the machine well oiled. If a major problem does occur, knitters may call in a specialist to repair the machine.

Knit goods workers are also needed in other areas of the production process. They prepare the yarn before it goes to the knitters and then clean and wash the fabric after it has gone through the machines. Many fabrics are then dyed with color or given special finishes to make them waterproof or wrinkle-resistant. All of the above operations are usually done by machine, but workers must mix the chemicals and watch the machines.

After the production process is completed, workers inspect the fabrics to make sure there are no flaws. Then they press the material and box it for shipping. Different workers usually handle these tasks, but in small companies the same worker may do a variety of tasks.

Education and Training

Although a high school diploma is not always required for jobs in this industry, it is highly recommended. Take classes in art, computer science, family and consumer science, math, and English.

The best way to become a knit goods industry worker is to complete an apprenticeship program offered by textile manufacturers. These programs last from several days (for cleaners) to several months (for machine repairers). Apprenticeships include on-the-job training and courses in math and machine shop practice. Many community colleges and technical schools also offer two-year programs in textile making.

Although a college degree is not necessary for most jobs in this field, those who wish to become designers or production managers usually need a college degree as well as several years of work experience. Workers can also advance through company-sponsored training programs. Some may go on to become instructors themselves.

DID YOU KNOW?

- In 2008, the textile, textile product, and apparel manufacturing industries provided approximately 497,100 wage and salary jobs.
- Forty-four percent of people in these industries work in California, Georgia, and North Carolina.
- Most workers are employed at companies of 50 workers or more.
- Production workers make up approximately 66 percent of workers in the apparel industry.

Source: U.S. Department of Labor

Earnings

The earnings of knit goods workers vary according to the location of the mill they work in and the goods they produce. The U.S. Department of Labor reports that the median annual earnings for textile knitting and weaving machine setters, operators, and tenders were $25,650 in 2009. Those just starting out in the field made less than $18,000 a year. Very experienced workers earned more than $34,000. Textile cutting machine setters, operators, and tenders earned $23,600 a year in 2009. Many production workers in apparel manufacturing are paid according to the number of pieces they produce, so their total earnings depend on their skill, speed, and

FOR MORE INFO

For information on the latest fashion market trends and news in the industry, contact
American Apparel and Footwear Association
http://www.apparelandfootwear.org

For information on the manufactured fibers knit goods industry, contact
American Fiber Manufacturers Association
1530 Wilson Boulevard, Suite 690
Arlington, VA 22209-2418
703-875-0432
http://www.afma.org

For news and general industry information, contact
National Council of Textile Organizations
910 17th Street, NW, Suite 1020
Washington, DC 20006-2623

202-822-8028
http://www.ncto.org

This union fights for workers' rights. It represents workers in various industries, including apparel and textiles. Check out the UNITE HERE! Web site to read about campaigns to stop sweatshops, where to purchase union-made apparel, and more.
UNITE HERE!
275 7th Avenue
New York, NY 10001-6708
212-265-7000
http://www.unitehere.org

For career information, visit
Career Threads
http://careerthreads.com

accuracy. Apprentices are normally paid wages that are lower than those of experienced employees. These wages rise as they gain experience.

Outlook

Employment prospects for knit goods workers and other textile workers are not expected to be strong. In fact, there will be a rapid decline in employment for knitting industry workers in coming years. While the demand for knit goods has increased along with population growth, automation and overseas production have combined to keep the demand for knit goods workers low in the United States. The number of jobs in knitting mills has decreased significantly because plants have closed or downsized.

Labor-saving, computerized machinery has increased productivity. Job prospects look best for skilled engineers, technicians, computer personnel, and others who know how to use and service complex knitting machinery.

Makeup Artists

What Makeup Artists Do

Makeup artists apply makeup to actors and models. They are employed in the fashion, motion picture, and television and commercial industries. They also work in theatrical productions.

Makeup artists who work in the fashion industry prepare models for photo shoots, fashion shows, and other fashion industry events. They often work closely with designers to create makeup and hair "looks" for seasonal collections. In addition to applying makeup, in smaller markets, makeup artists are often responsible for styling hair, extensions, and wigs.

Makeup artists play an important role during fashion events as well. For example, they observe models during fashion shows to make sure their makeup is just right. They reapply or adjust makeup as needed during the show. They help the models remove makeup at the end of the day. These artists must be able to spot any makeup problems before a fashion show or other event begins.

EXPLORING

- Read *The Artisan* magazine (http://www.local706.org/ artisan.cfm) to learn about makeup artists who work in the film and television industries.
- Look for opportunities to volunteer your help to local theaters. The summer months will offer the most opportunities. Small community theaters will pay little or nothing, but they may allow you the best chance to explore makeup artistry.
- Volunteer to do makeup for school productions or fashion shows. Make sure to take pictures of your work.
- Talk with a makeup artist about his or her work.

A makeup artist applies makeup to a model. (Jeff Christensen, AP Photo)

Makeup artists also design and apply makeup for stage and screen actors. They read scripts and meet with directors, producers, and special effects technicians. They create makeup and special effects such as scars and prosthetics (artificial body parts). Sometimes makeup artists apply "clean" (natural-looking) makeup and eliminate or apply wrinkles, tattoos, or scars. When they design makeup, makeup artists must consider the age of the characters, the setting and period of the film or play, and the lighting effects that will be used. Historical productions require considerable research to design hair, makeup, and fashion styles of a particular era. Makeup artists also may work on hair, but in many states locally licensed cosmetologists must be brought in for hair cutting, coloring, and perms.

Most makeup artists are self-employed and work on a freelance basis. Makeup artists for the theater may be employed full-time by a theater, or they may be freelancers. Freelance makeup artists must handle all the administrative tasks that go with running a business. These include arranging job appointments, running errands, invoicing clients, updating their portfolio and Web sites, and shopping for supplies in stores and online.

Education and Training

Most makeup artists have bachelor's or master's degrees in theater, art history, film history, photography, fashion merchandising, fashion, or a related subject. To prepare for a career as a makeup artist, take art classes, such as art history, photography, painting, drawing, and sculpting. Anatomy and chemistry

Profile: Rick Baker (1950–   )

Rick Baker is considered one of the best makeup artists in Hollywood. As a child, he was a fan of horror movies. He experimented with movie makeup effects as a teen, and landed his first professional job assisting the famous makeup artist Dick Smith on *The Exorcist.*

In 1981, when the Best Makeup category was introduced, Rick Baker received an Oscar for his work on *An American Werewolf in London.* He also won Oscars for his work on the following films: *Harry and the Hendersons* (1987), *Ed Wood* (1994), *The Nutty Professor* (1996), *Men in Black* (1997), and *Dr. Seuss' How the Grinch Stole Christmas* (2000). In 2009, he received the Jack Pierce-Lifetime Achievement Award. Jack Pierce was a pioneering makeup artist in the early days of Hollywood.

Sources: Filmreference.com, About.com

classes will also be useful. Some high schools offer courses in fashion; if available, take as many as possible. Participate in school drama productions, and assist with makeup whenever possible.

Cosmetology licenses or certificates from special makeup schools are not required, but they may help, especially when you start out. If you are willing to spend some time working for very little pay, or even for free, you can gain valuable experience assisting an experienced, established makeup artist. There are also some highly regarded schools for makeup artists, such as the Joe Blasco Makeup Schools in California and Florida.

Tips for Success

To be a successful makeup artist, you should

- have patience
- be able to work well with others
- have artistic ability
- be attentive to detail
- be able to work well under deadline pressure
- have business skills
- be able to accept constructive criticism regarding your work
- be confident of your abilities

Earnings

Makeup artists usually earn a daily rate for their services. This rate varies depending on the budget and size of the production and the experience and reputation of the makeup artist. Day rates can range from $50 for a small theater production to $1,000 for a large Broadway show or feature film. Work is rarely steady. Most makeup artists work long hours for several weeks, and then may be without work for a time.

The U.S. Department of Labor reports that makeup artists, theatrical and performance who worked full time had median annual salaries of $31,450 in 2009. Salaries ranged from less than $17,000 to more than $94,000. However, celebrity artists can earn salaries of more than $100,000.

FOR MORE INFO

For information on union membership, contact
International Alliance of Theatrical Stage Employees, Moving Picture Technicians, Artists and Allied Crafts of the United States, Its Territories, and Canada
1430 Broadway, 20th Floor
New York, NY 10018-3348
212-730-1770
http://www.iatse-intl.org

This local union represents the professional interests of makeup artists and hair stylists who work in film and television. Visit its Web site for more information.

Make-Up Artists & Hair Stylists Guild Local 706
http://www.local706.org

For information on theatrical careers, contact
Theatre Communications Group
520 Eighth Avenue, 24th Floor
New York, NY 10018-4156
212-609-5900
tcg@tcg.org
http://www.tcg.org

For information about the Joe Blasco Makeup Schools and careers in makeup artistry, visit
Joe Blasco Makeup Schools
http://www.joeblasco.com

Outlook

Employment opportunities for makeup artists vary by specialty. It will be difficult to land a job working solely in the fashion industry because the field is so small and many people want to enter it. New jobs will become available as the film and television industries continue to grow. Increased use of special effects will require makeup artists with special talent and training. On the other hand, the growing popularity of computer-generated effects in films and television shows will reduce the number of makeup artists needed for some productions. The future for work in theaters is less predictable, but traveling productions and regional theaters should continue to offer employment opportunities. Makeup artists with advanced training, strong artistic skills, and the ability to find work in multiple industries will have the best job prospects.

Merchandise Displayers

What Merchandise Displapers Do

Merchandise displayers design and build displays for store windows, showcases, and floors. They are sometimes called *display workers, showcase trimmers,* and *window dressers.* Store displays must be artistic and attractive so that customers will want to buy the products.

Some merchandise displayers work in self-service stores, such as supermarkets. Because there are no salespeople, displays are very important in attracting the customer to buy products. In large retail stores, such as department stores, there may be a large staff of display specialists. These workers often use mannequins and other props for displaying apparel (clothing). Merchandise displayers also prepare product displays for trade shows, exhibitions, conventions, or festivals. They build installations such as booths and exhibits. They also install carpeting, drapes, and other decorations, including flags, banners, and lights, and arrange furniture and other accessories.

Displayers first develop an idea or theme that will highlight the merchandise and attract customers. Display workers use hammers, saws, spray guns, and other hand tools to build displays. They may use carpeting, wallpaper, and special lighting. They build and paint the backdrops and gather all the props they'll need. Finally, they arrange merchandise and hang printed materials, such as signs, descriptions of the merchandise, and price tags.

Sometimes display workers work in teams where each worker has a specialty, such as sign making, window painting, or carpentry.

73

EXPLORING

- You can find lots of opportunities to work on displays at school. Ask your teachers if you can help design and arrange bulletin boards, posters, or displays for special events, such as parents' night and fund-raisers.
- Participate in groups that are in charge of decorations or publicity for school dances and parties.
- Join your school or community drama group to work on sets, props, and costumes.
- Help your neighbors arrange items for garage or yard sales.
- Take art, sculpture, calligraphy, or carpentry courses offered in your community.
- Once you enter high school, try to land a job as a clerk or merchandise display assistant at a clothing or department store.
- Talk to a merchandise displayer about his or her career.

Most merchandise displayers work in clothing and department stores. Others are employed in other types of retail stores—such as drug, variety, and shoe stores—or for design firms that are hired to do window dressing for small stores. Some merchandise displayers are self-employed.

Education and Training

Merchandise displayers must have at least a high school education. Courses in art, woodworking, mechanical drawing, and merchandising are useful. Some employers expect their merchandise displayers to have taken college courses in art, fashion merchandising, advertising, and interior decorating.

A merchandise displayer sets up a mannequin at a fashion boutique.
(Ng Han Guan, AP Photo)

Tips for Success

To be a successful merchandise displayer, you should

- be creative
- have manual dexterity and mechanical aptitude
- have good physical strength and physical ability
- have excellent communication skills
- be able to work well as a member of a team
- be able to follow instructions

Art institutes, colleges and universities, and some junior colleges offer courses in merchandise display and fashion merchandising. Typical classes in a fashion merchandising program include Merchandising Principles and Practices, Visual Merchandising, Merchandise Planning and Inventory Control, Fashion Marketing and Consumer Behavior, Project Management in Merchandising, Introduction to Fashion, Trend Forecasting, and Fashion Publicity and Promotion. Students also complete a fashion merchandising internship or capstone project.

Many merchandise displayers receive their training on the job. They may start as sales clerks and learn while assisting window dressers or display workers.

Earnings

According to the U.S. Department of Labor, merchandise displayers earned a median yearly salary of $25,970 in 2009. Merchandise displayers who worked in department stores had mean annual earnings of $27,560, while those who worked at clothing stores earned $27,380. New displayers earned $18,000 or less. Very experienced displayers earned more than $42,000 a year. Freelancers may earn as much as $50,000 a year, but their income depends on their reputation,

DID YOU KNOW?

Approximately 85,200 merchandise displayers and window trimmers were employed in the United States in 2008, according to the U.S. Department of Labor.

FOR MORE INFO

This organization offers information on becoming an interior designer (a field that is related to merchandise display), including school listings and details on career specialties.

American Society of Interior Designers
608 Massachusetts Avenue, NE
Washington, DC 20002-6006
202-546-3480
http://www.asid.org

The institute works with colleges and universities to develop retail design programs. Visit its Web site for information on retail design.

Retail Design Institute
25 North Broadway
Tarrytown, NY 10590-3221
800-379-9912
info@retaildesigninstitute.org
http://www.retaildesigninstitute.org

To read about industry news and see the latest design ideas, check out the following magazine's Web site:

Display & Design Ideas Magazine
http://www.ddionline.com/display anddesignideas/index.shtml

number of clients, and number of hours they work. Display workers in big-city stores earn more that those employed by stores in smaller towns.

Outlook

Employment for merchandise displayers should be good during the next decade. The number of retail stores continues to grow, and they will need merchandisers to help sell products. Most openings will occur as older, experienced workers retire or leave the field. Merchandise displayers with advanced education and experience will have the best job prospects.

Personal Shoppers

What Personal Shoppers Do

People who don't have the time or the ability to go shopping for clothes, gifts, groceries, and other items use the services of *personal shoppers*. Personal shoppers shop at department stores, look at catalogs, and search the Internet for the best buys and most appropriate items for their clients.

Personal shoppers help people who are unable to shop or who are uninterested in doing their own shopping. For example, they might do grocery shopping and run other errands for senior citizens or people with disabilities. Shoppers may also help professionals create an appropriate, complete business wardrobe. Whatever the shopping assignment, they rely on their knowledge of the local marketplace in order to shop quickly and efficiently.

Some personal shoppers specialize in a particular area. For example, someone with a background in cosmetology or fashion may work as an *image consultant,* advising clients on their hair, clothes, and makeup and shopping for clothing and beauty products.

Personal shoppers who offer wardrobe consultation visit their clients' homes and evaluate their clothes. Shoppers help determine what additional clothes and accessories they need (such as a new business suit, ties, or shoes) and offer advice on what items to wear together. With their clients, personal shoppers come up with a budget and start shopping at stores or on the Internet.

Personal shoppers also buy gifts for clients who don't have the time to shop themselves. Shoppers may get very specific

EXPLORING

- Go to a mall and study other people's buying habits. Do people linger longer in certain stores? Do they try on a lot of items only to walk out? Think of ways you could make the shopping experience easier for people with limited time.
- Learn about budgeting, comparison pricing, and negotiating.
- If you are old enough to apply for a part-time job, consider working at a retail store to learn more about selling merchandise and assisting customers.
- Offer to shop for a family member or an elderly person in your community. Once you find out what they need to buy (clothing, food, etc.), try to find the best deal for them by searching the Internet and visiting stores in your area.
- Before you go spending other people's money, you should have a good sense of your own. Check out these books to learn money-saving tips and become master of your own bank account: *The Everything Kids' Money Book: Earn It, Save It, and Watch It Grow!*, 2d ed., by Brette McWhorter Sember (Adams Media Corporation, 2008); *The New Totally Awesome Money Book for Kids*, 3d ed., by Arthur Bochner (Newmarket, 2007); and *Money Sense for Kids*, 2d ed., by Hollis Page Harman (Barron's Educational Series, 2005).
- Visit the following Web site to learn more about money and financial management: Kids & Money (http://www.ext.nodak.edu/extnews/pipeline/d-parent.htm).

instructions on what to purchase, or they may have to think of gift ideas themselves after talking with the client and discussing the recipient's tastes. Some shoppers run other errands, such as purchasing theater tickets, making deliveries, dropping off laundry, and going to the post office.

Most personal shoppers are self-employed, but some work for department stores that provide personal shopping services. Others work for companies that provide these services to businesses or individuals.

Education and Training

Take classes in family and consumer science to develop budget and consumer skills as well as learn about fashion and design. Math, business, and accounting courses will prepare you for the administrative details of the job. Any courses that teach you how to manage money and negotiate will also be useful.

Many people working as personal shoppers have had experience in other areas of business. They've worked as managers in corporations or as salespeople in retail clothing stores. But there isn't any specific education or training required for this career. A small-business course at a local community college, along with classes in design, fashion, and consumer science, can help you develop the skills you'll need for the job.

Tips for Success

To be a successful personal shopper, you should

- have excellent communication skills
- be able to follow instructions
- be motivated to help your clients find the best products at the lowest prices possible
- have good negotiation skills
- be willing to travel often as part of your job
- be a good researcher
- be patient to deal with long lines at stores and other challenges
- be creative and able to come up with a variety of gift ideas
- have a sense of style

Earnings

Personal shoppers bill their clients in different ways: They set a regular fee for services, charge a percentage of the sale, or charge an hourly rate. Or,

Helping Hands: Blake Mycoskie and TOMS Shoes

Many children in developing countries are so poor they do not have any shoes to wear. As a result, these children often suffer from cuts and fungus infections on their feet. Others are not allowed to go to school because footwear is part of the school's dress code. There are also children, because they share a single pair of shoes with siblings, who are forced to attend school only every other day—when it is their turn to wear the shoes.

After learning about the plight of these children, entrepreneur Blake Mycoskie knew he had to do something. He founded the organization TOMS Shoes. Banking on the purchasing power of individuals, Mycoskie sells shoes using the "one for one" model. This means that for every pair of shoes sold, TOMS Shoes donates a pair to a needy child. The shoes, which are designed similar to espadrilles (shoes with a fabric top and a flexible bottom made of rubber or rope), come in a variety of colors and designs.

Since its start, TOMS Shoes has donated more than 600,000 pairs of shoes to needy children in many countries, including Guatemala, Argentina, Haiti, and Rwanda, as well as in poor areas of the United States. The company uses shoe drops—a project that includes traveling to a country, getting children properly fitted, and hand delivering their brand-new shoes.

Mycoskie's vision has gained momentum. Many designers, manufacturers, celebrities, even college campuses, have joined the cause by donating their skills, participating in shoe drops, or creating limited edition styles. Once a year, TOMS Shoes calls for "A Day Without Shoes," and encourages the public to go about their daily activities without the comfort and protection of footwear. This helps people understand the challenges of not having shoes.

Blake Mycoskie is a great example of someone who sees a wrong in the world and tries to fix it. Because of his work, poor children around the world are living better lives.

Sources: *The Huffington Post,*
Toms.com

FOR MORE INFO

This organization represents the professional interests of image consultants, a career field that is a specialty of personal shoppers. Visit its Web site for more information about the field.

Association of Image Consultants International
100 East Grand Avenue, Suite 330
Des Moines, IA 50309-1835
515-282-5500
info@aici.org
http://www.aici.org

they might use all these methods in their business. Their billing method may depend on the client and the service. For example, when offering wardrobe consultation and shopping for clothes, a personal shopper may find it best to charge by the hour; when shopping for a small gift, it may be more reasonable to charge only a percentage. Personal shoppers charge anywhere from $25 to $125 an hour. The average hourly rate is about $75. Successful shoppers working in large cities can make between $1,500 and $4,000 a month.

Outlook

As our society becomes busier, people have less time for shopping and errands. This is good news for personal shoppers. Personal shopping is fairly new, so anyone starting out in this career will find it challenging to obtain clients and build their business. The success of Internet commerce will probably have a big effect on the future of personal shopping. Some personal shoppers who have Web sites offer consultation via e-mail and help people purchase products online.

Photo Stylists

What Photo Stylists Do

Photo stylists work with photographers, art directors, models, and clients to create visual images. They use props, backgrounds, accessories, food, linens, clothing, costumes, and other set elements to create these images. Much of the work they do is for catalogs and newspaper and magazine advertising. Stylists also work on films and television commercials.

Most stylists specialize in fashion, food, hair and makeup, or bridal styling. Some do only prop shopping or location searches. Prop shopping involves searching local stores and resale shops for props (such as furniture, dinnerware, etc.) that will be used in advertisements. Location searches are conducted to find the right spot for an advertising shoot or commercial to be filmed. Others photo stylists prefer to develop a variety of skills so they can find different kinds of photo styling work.

Photo stylists use their imagination, resourcefulness, and artistic skills to set up a shot that will help sell a product. For example, a mail-order clothing company may want a series of ads to sell their winter line of clothing. Photo stylists may decide to design a set outside with a snow background or indoors near a fireplace with holiday decorations in the background. They gather props, such as lamps or table decorations. They rent chairs and couches to decorate the set where the shoot will take place. For an outdoor scene, they might use a sled or skiing equipment. Photo stylists hire models to wear the clothing. They may work with other photo stylists and assistants to style the hair and makeup of the models.

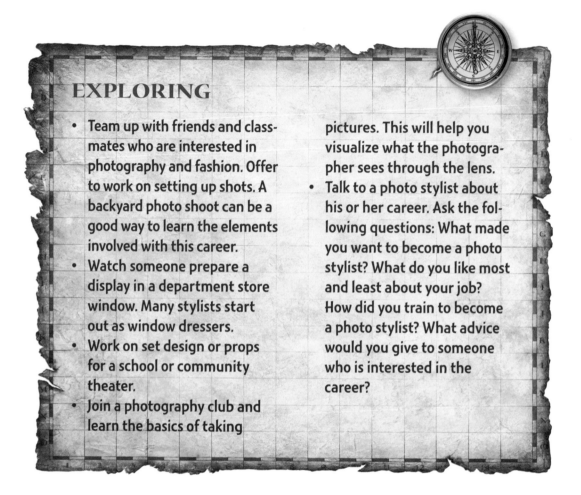

EXPLORING

- Team up with friends and classmates who are interested in photography and fashion. Offer to work on setting up shots. A backyard photo shoot can be a good way to learn the elements involved with this career.
- Watch someone prepare a display in a department store window. Many stylists start out as window dressers.
- Work on set design or props for a school or community theater.
- Join a photography club and learn the basics of taking pictures. This will help you visualize what the photographer sees through the lens.
- Talk to a photo stylist about his or her career. Ask the following questions: What made you want to become a photo stylist? What do you like most and least about your job? How did you train to become a photo stylist? What advice would you give to someone who is interested in the career?

Photo stylists usually have a "bag of tricks" that will solve problems or create certain visual effects. This kit may include everything from duct tape to cotton wadding to a spare saltshaker. Sometimes photo stylists build and design props from scratch. They may have to oversee the entire production, from finding the location to arranging places to stay for the crew. The best photo stylists are versatile and creative enough to come up with ideas and solutions on the spot. If they cannot create or locate something, they have many contacts that can help them out.

Photo stylists must be organized. They must make sure to gather everything that they need for a photo shoot and be sure that all materials are well cared for. After the shoot, photo stylists make sure that all borrowed items are returned and that all rentals and other transactions have been recorded.

Education and Training

There is no specific training or schooling to become a photo stylist, but there are other ways to prepare for this job. Art classes can help train your eye for design and composition. Experience with building and constructing displays will be of great help. Sewing skills are necessary, especially in fashion photo design, to make minor alterations to fabrics. Those interested in hair and makeup styling should take courses in cosmetology. Interior design courses will help you learn how to arrange room

DID YOU KNOW?

Where Photo Stylists Work

- Advertising agencies
- Any companies that sell their merchandise through catalogs
- Catalog houses
- Design firms
- Magazine publishers
- Self-employment

Tools of the Trade

Following are some of the things photo stylists might carry with them to photo shoots:

- Blow torch
- Brushes
- Cloth steamer
- Cotton swabs
- Eye droppers
- Glycerine
- Mixer
- Needle and thread
- Oil
- Pastry bags and tips
- Safety pins
- Skewers
- Spray bottles
- Tape
- Toothpicks
- Tweezers
- Utility knife

FOR MORE INFO

To view the work of photo stylists, visit
Photo Talent Online
http://www.phototalentonline.com

This organization provides training, publishes its own magazine, and offers various services for its members.
Professional Photographers of America
229 Peachtree Street, NE, Suite 2200
Atlanta, GA 30303-1608
Tel: 800-786-6277
http://www.ppa.com

settings. A general knowledge of photography, film, and lighting will help you communicate with photographers.

Most photo stylists enter the field as apprentices to established stylists. Apprentices usually work for two years or more before taking on clients on their own.

Earnings

Salaries at production houses can start as low as $8 an hour. Experienced fashion or food stylists can earn as much as $800 a day and more, depending on reputation and the budget of the production. On average, stylists earn around $350 to $500 per day as freelancers. According to the Association of Stylists and Coordinators, assistant photo stylists earn about $150 to $200 a day.

Outlook

Employment of photo stylists is expected to grow at an average rate. Good photo stylists are becoming more and more important to photographers and advertising clients. However, the employment outlook of photo stylists depends on the health of the advertising, film, and commercial photography industries.

New digital photography and photo enhancement technology may change the role of the photo stylist in the future. There may be more educational programs for photo stylists and this may increase the competition for styling assignments.

Retail Managers and Business Owners

What Retail Managers and Business Owners Do

Retail managers make sure that stores run smoothly. *Retail business owners* start or buy their own businesses or franchise operations.

Retail managers and owners not only work in clothing stores, but they also work in supermarkets, department stores, gift shops, bakeries, and any other type of shop. But because this book deals with fashion careers, the focus here will be on clothing store managers and owners.

Managers are in charge of everything that takes place in the store, from hiring and managing employees to ensuring that displayed clothes are neatly folded and attractively arranged. They also handle the money that is made in the shop. They make sure that all receipts are tallied up, cash in the register is counted, and all is put safely away at the end of each working day. The manager is often the first to arrive in the morning and the last to leave at night.

The most important skill for a good retail manager is knowing how to work with other people. Managers hire and train employees, assign their duties, and review salaries. There are bound to be disagreements and clashes from time to time. Managers must be able to keep arguments from getting out of control. Similarly, the store's customers may have complaints, and managers must be sensitive and understanding in dealing with the public.

EXPLORING

- Check out the Web site of *STORES* (http://www.stores. org), which is published by the National Retail Federation. The site includes industry statistics, sales trends, and other articles on the retail field. Although it is geared toward adults, browsing it can give you a good idea of important issues in the field.
- Test out your retail sales skills by working at your local mall. If you are too young for part-time work, ask if you can volunteer to help out.
- Any retail experience would be beneficial. Volunteer to work at a sales booth at a school event such as a play, bake sale, or basketball game.
- Talk to retail managers and business owners about their careers.

Whether they deal in clothing, shoes, or accessories, retail managers track all the merchandise in their stores. They keep accurate records so they know when to order new items, which items are the most popular, and which items are not selling.

Some managers handle all advertising and product promotions themselves, while others meet with advertising agency representatives and decide how best to advertise their store's merchandise. Managers often have the final say about which advertisements are sent to newspapers, radio, and television, or posted online.

Other duties vary depending on the size of the store and the type of merchandise sold. In small stores, managers perform such duties as data processing, shipping, accounting, and sales. In large stores, managers may be responsible for a specific area, such as customer service or personnel.

Retail business owners are responsible for all aspects of a business operation, from planning and ordering merchandise to overseeing day-to-day operations. There are five general job categories in retail establishments: merchandising and buying, store operations, sales promotion and advertising, bookkeeping and accounting, and personnel supervision. Retail business owners must know about all five of these areas in order to make informed business decisions. Specific duties of an owner depend on the size of the store and the number of employees. In a store with more than 10 employees, many of the day-to-day operation, promotion, and personnel activities are supervised by managers, while the owner plans the overall purpose and function of the store. In a smaller store, the owner may handle most of these jobs, including sweeping the floor, greeting customers, balancing the accounting books, and placing ads in newspapers.

In both large and small operations, an owner has to keep up-to-date on product information as well as economic and technological conditions that may impact a business. Owners read catalogs about products, check current inventories and prices, and research any technological advances that may make the store more efficient.

Franchise owners obtain a license to sell an existing company's goods or services. The license agreement allows them to use expert advice from the sponsoring company about location, hiring and training of employees, arrangement of merchandise, advertising, and record keeping.

Education and Training

Although some retail managers do not have a college education, many large retail stores accept applications only from college graduates. If you are interested in this career, study English, advertising, accounting, math, business, and marketing in high school. All managers, regardless of their education, must have good marketing, analytical, and people skills.

The owner of an upscale women's clothing boutique poses with some of her sales goods. (Michael Kubel, AP Photo/*The Morning Call*)

Many large retail stores and national chains offer formal training programs, including classroom instruction, for their new employees. The training period may last a week or as long as a year. Training for a department store manager, for example, may include working as a salesperson in several departments in order to learn more about the store's business.

Part-time or summer jobs are good ways to enter this field. Often retail managers are looking for salespeople because the turnover rate in these jobs is quite high. A salesperson who stays with a company and takes increasing responsibility is more likely to advance into a management position.

There are no specific educational or experience requirements for retail business owners. High school courses in math, business management, accounting, typing, and computer science are helpful. Experience in the retail trade is recommended.

If you hope to own your own business someday, you are advised to earn a college degree. Recommended majors include business communications, marketing, business law, business management, and accounting. You may want to earn a master's in business administration or a degree in a related field such as sales or marketing. There are also special business schools that offer one- or two-year programs in business management. Some correspondence schools also offer courses on how to plan and run a business.

Tips for Success

To be a successful retail manager or owner, you should

- have excellent communication skills
- be good at managing and motivating people
- be willing to put in very long hours
- be responsible
- have a calm personality and be able to handle stress
- be highly ethical

Earnings

Salaries for retail managers depend on the size of the retail store, the responsibilities of the job, and the number of customers served. According to the U.S. Department of Labor, mean annual earnings of supervisors of retail sales workers, including commission, in clothing stores were $39,130 in 2009. Managers who worked in department stores earned $32,190. Salaries for all retail managers ranged from less than $22,000 to more than $61,000 per year. Managers who oversee an entire region for a retail chain can earn more than $100,000.

In addition to a salary, some stores offer their managers special bonuses, or commissions. These are typically connected to

DID YOU KNOW?

The Gap is the largest (by revenue) apparel chain in the United States, according to STORES magazine. Other large apparel chains (in descending order) include Limited Brands, Ross Stores, Burlington Coat Factory, Abercrombie & Fitch, American Eagle Outfitters, Charming Shoppes, Liz Claiborne Direct Brands, Ann Taylor Stores, Men's Wearhouse, and Polo Ralph Lauren.

the store's performance. Many managers also receive employee discounts on store merchandise.

Earnings for retail business owners vary greatly based on the location of the store, its size, the type of goods sold, and other factors. Some retail business owners may earn less than $15,000 a year, while the most successful owners earn $150,000 or more.

Outlook

Employment for retail managers is expected to be only fair through the next decade. Although fashion retailers have reduced their management staff to cut costs and make operations more efficient, there still are good opportunities in retailing. However, competition for jobs probably will continue to increase, and computerized systems for inventory control may reduce the need for some types of managers. Applicants with the best educational backgrounds and work experience will have the strongest chances of finding jobs.

The retail field is extremely competitive, and many businesses fail each year. An uncertain economy can lead to retail bankruptcies, mergers, and downsizings. Increasing unemployment, the weakening of consumer confidence, increased competition from other retailers and direct marketers, and the growth of Internet businesses are just some of the issues retail business owners will face in the next decade.

FOR MORE INFO

Visit the association's Web site for comprehensive information regarding franchising.

International Franchise Association
1501 K Street, NW, Suite 350
Washington, DC 20005-1412
202-628-8000
http://www.franchise.org

For information on educational programs and careers in the retail industry, contact

National Retail Federation
325 7th Street, NW, Suite 1100
Washington, DC 20004-2825
800-673-4692
http://www.nrf.com

For information on jobs in retail, contact
Retail Industry Leaders Association
1700 North Moore Street, Suite 2250
Arlington, VA 22209-1933
703-841-2300
http://www.rila.org

Retail Sales Workers

EXPLORING

- Read books about fashion and retail.
- Visit http://www.pbs.org/news hour/on2/fashion.html to read about the origins of fashion and browse other fun articles.
- Look for opportunities to develop your customer service skills. Volunteer to work at a hospital gift shop or work a ticket booth at your next school play.
- Once you are in high school, try to get a job as a sales worker at a clothing or department store.
- Participate in fund-raising activities, such as bake sales, candy sales, and rummage sales.
- Talk to a retail sales worker about his or her career.

What Retail Sales Workers Do

Retail sales workers assist customers in retail stores. In the fashion world, they help customers decide what clothes, shoes, and other wearable accessories to buy and oversee fitting rooms, where customers try on clothing. They ring up sales and take payment. Some other names for retail sales workers are *sales clerks, retail clerks,* and *salespeople.*

A retail sales worker may have a wide range of duties. In a small retail store, the sales worker may take inventory (count the number of items that are in stock), place newspaper ads, order and price apparel (clothing), fold or hang clothes, answer telephone calls, open the store in the morning, and lock it up at night. In a large department store, retail sales workers usually work in one department (such as junior fashions) and have more limited duties.

The main job of most retail sales workers is to help customers. They help find the specific items customers want or suggest alternate choices. They may help customers put outfits together, fetch new sizes, and recommend certain brands or looks. When they are not waiting on customers, retail workers put price tags on items, stock the store, straighten clothes shelves and racks, clean products, and make sure aisles are clear.

With good skills, retail sales workers can move up to any of several positions. Some become the *senior salesperson* or a *department head.* They manage the other employees in the department and may be responsible for placing orders for new merchandise. With experience, retail workers can also become floor managers, branch managers, and general managers. Some sales workers move on to become *buyers,* who decide what clothing and other merchandise the store will carry and purchase these items. (For more info, see Buyers.) Others may eventually own their own stores. (See Retail Managers and Business Owners.)

Some retail sales workers have a 40-hour workweek. In many stores, however, sales workers work 44 or 48 hours a week. Working on evenings and weekends is often required, as is working long hours of overtime during the holiday seasons, when stores are the busiest. Workers in many stores have to stay past closing time to clean up the sales floor after a busy day.

Education and Training

In high school, take courses in business, English, speech, and math. Some high schools have special programs that include courses in merchandising, principles of retailing, and retail selling.

Employers generally hire retail workers who are at least high school graduates, although there are part-time opportunities available to high school students. Entry-level employees sometimes are asked to work in the store's stockroom at first so that they can learn more about the store's products and operations. They also may be asked to help set up displays or assist in the

A sales clerk wheels a rack of men's shirts down an aisle in preparation for restocking. (Stephan Savoia, AP Photo)

customer service department. After several months they may be promoted to sales workers.

Many employers prefer to hire college graduates, especially those with degrees in merchandising, business, or liberal arts. College graduates are more likely to be put directly into the store's management training program. Job applicants with previous retail sales experience also are considered good candidates to become managers.

DID YOU KNOW?

- Nearly 4.5 million people are employed as sales workers in retail stores of all types and sizes.
- Approximately 34 percent of retail sales workers are employed part time.
- Twenty-nine percent of workers at clothing, accessory, and general merchandise stores are 23 years of age or younger.

Source: U.S. Department of Labor

Earnings

Most beginning sales workers start at the federal minimum wage, which is $7.25 an hour. Wages vary greatly, depending mainly on the size and type of store and the degree of skill required. Larger retail stores might be able to offer higher wages to attract and keep their best workers.

According to the U.S. Department of Labor, median earnings of all retail salespersons, including commission, were $20,260 in 2009. Salaries ranged from less than $16,000 to more than $38,000. Sales workers in department stores earned an average of $21,000. In clothing stores, they earned $21,210.

Department stores or retail chains might pay more than smaller stores. Many sales workers also receive a commission (a portion of the total amount of merchandise sold—often 4 to 8 percent) on their sales or are paid solely on commission.

A Famous Name

Some people buy clothes just for the label that is on it. What is one of the most popular labels? Ralph Lauren. Not bad for a guy who never went to school for fashion design. He got into his line of work as a sales worker!

FOR MORE INFO

For information on educational programs and careers in the retail industry, contact
National Retail Federation
325 7th Street, NW, Suite 1100
Washington, DC 20004-2825
800-673-4692
http://www.nrf.com

Salespeople in many retail stores receive a discount on their own purchases, ranging from 10 to 25 percent. This privilege is sometimes also extended to the worker's family.

Outlook

Employment for sales personnel will be good during the next decade. Turnover among sales workers is much higher than average, creating a continual need to replace workers.

There should continue to be good opportunities for temporary and part-time sales workers, especially during the holidays. Stores are particularly interested in people who, by returning year after year, develop good sales backgrounds and know the store's merchandise.

Tailors and Dressmakers

What Tailors and Dressmakers Do

Tailors and dressmakers cut, sew, mend, and alter clothing. Most tailors work with menswear, such as suits, jackets, and coats. Dressmakers typically work with women's clothing, such as dresses, suits, evening wear, and wedding clothes. Tailors and dressmakers may work for dressmaking and custom tailor shops, department stores, dry cleaners, and garment factories. Many others are self-employed. They run a small shop or take in jobs at home.

Some tailors and dressmakers specialize in custom clothing and make garments from start to finish. They help customers choose the style and fabric, using their knowledge of the various types of fabrics. They take the customer's measurements, such as height, shoulder width, and arm length. Tailors and dressmakers may use ready-made paper patterns, though many are trained to make their own. The patterns are then placed on the fabric, and the fabric pieces are carefully cut. If the pattern is a difficult one, or if there are special fitting problems, the tailor or dressmaker may cut the pattern from muslin (cotton

EXPLORING

- Read books about the field.
- Take sewing classes at school. Your local park district or fabric and craft stores often offer lessons year-round.
- Create and sew your own designs or offer your mending and alteration services to your family and friends.
- Visit department stores, clothing specialty stores, and tailors' shops to observe workers involved in this field.

99

A tailor takes a customer's measurements. (Vincent Yu, AP Photo)

fabric) and fit it to the customer. Adjustments are made and transferred to the paper pattern before it is used to cut the actual fabric. The cut pieces are basted (temporarily sewn) together first and then sewn by hand or machine. Fittings are held to make sure the garment fits the customer properly. Afterward the garment is finished with hems, buttons, trim, and a final pressing.

Tailors and dressmakers who work at larger shops may be trained to specialize in a specific task such as patternmaking, cutting, fitting, or sewing. *Bushelers* work in factories to repair flaws and correct imperfect sewing in finished garments. *Shop tailors* have a detailed knowledge of special tailoring tasks. They use shears (a cutting tool) or a knife to trim and shape the edges of garments before sewing, attach shoulder pads, and sew lining in coats. *Skilled tailors,* also known as *custom tailors,* put fine stitching on lapels and pockets, make buttonholes, and sew on trim.

Workers in this field must obviously have the ability to sew very well (both by hand and machine), follow directions, and measure accurately. In addition to these skills, tailors and dressmakers must have a good eye for color and style. They need to know how to communicate with and satisfy customers. Strong interpersonal skills will help tailors and dressmakers get and keep clients.

Education and Training

To prepare for a career in this field, high school family and consumer science classes such as sewing and tailoring will be helpful. There are also many schools that offer on-site or home

Words to Learn: Types of Pins

Most modern pins are made of brass, nickel-plated steel, or stainless steel. There are different kinds of pins, each designed for a specific sewing purpose.

Ballpoint pins are designed to slide between fibers, so they are best suited for knits.

Dressmaker pins are considered all-purpose pins, though usually not used for fine materials such as silk. They have regular, glass, or plastic heads.

Pleating pins are designed for light- to medium-weight woven and knit fabrics.

Sequin pins are short and are primarily used for pinning sequins and beads.

Silk pins make only small puncture holes, so they are best suited for fine silk and synthetic materials.

Quilting pins are longer and heavier pins used for heavy, bulky fabrics.

T-pins are used for crafts and for pinning heavy fabrics. Their heads are long and flat, giving the pin a T shape.

DID YOU KNOW?

It took more than one individual's ingenuity to develop the greatest sewing invention of all time—the sewing machine.

Thomas Saint designed a machine in 1790 that could work with leather and canvas. However, he built only a patent model and never mass-produced his invention.

Barthelemy Thimonnier's invention, built in 1829, is considered the first practical sewing machine. Made entirely of wood, and using a barbed needle, this machine was able to sew a chain stitch (a group of looped stitches that form a chain). Thimonnier mass-produced his machines and was under contract with the French government to sew army uniforms. Local tailors, afraid of the competition, raided his shop and destroyed his sewing machines. Thimonnier was able to save one machine and fled to America.

Elias Howe is commonly credited with inventing the first practical sewing machine in 1844. He patented it in 1846. After marketing his machine abroad, Howe returned to America and found many other companies had infringed on his patent. He successfully sued.

Isaac Merrit Singer did much for the industry by mass-producing the sewing machine. He also allowed the public to purchase machines on credit and implemented an aggressive sales campaign. Singer Sewing Company is still in business today.

study courses in sewing and dressmaking. Some high schools even offer fashion-related courses. Math and art classes will teach you how to measure and draw sketches and designs.

Most tailors and dressmakers have at least a high school education. However, many employers prefer college graduates with advanced training in sewing, tailoring, draping, pattern-making, and design. A limited number of schools and colleges located in the United States offer this type of training. Consider enrolling in such programs, especially if you plan to expand your career from tailoring to design.

Many tailors and dressmakers receive their training from apprenticeships offered by custom tailor shops or garment manufacturers. Many others get their start from work in related jobs, such as an alterer in a custom tailoring shop or dry cleaner store.

Earnings

Salaries for tailors and dressmakers vary widely, depending on experience, skill, and location. The median annual salary for tailors, dressmakers, and custom sewers was $26,640 in 2009, according to the U.S. Department of Labor (DOL). The DOL reports the following mean annual earnings for tailors and dressmakers by employer in 2009: department stores, $34,090; clothing stores, $30,370; cut and sewn apparel manufacturing, $27,780; dry cleaning and laundry services, $25,910; and personal and household goods repair and maintenance, $24,680. Salaries for all tailors and dressmakers ranged from less than $18,000 to more than $41,000.

FOR MORE INFO

For information on careers in the apparel manufacturing industry, contact
American Apparel and Footwear Association
http://www.apparelandfootwear.org

Those interested in creating men's fashions should visit the CTDA Web site for business and training information.
Custom Tailors and Designers Association (CTDA)
42732 Ridgeway Drive
Broadlands, VA 20148-4558
888-248-2832
http://www.ctda.com

Outlook

Employment prospects in this industry are expected to decline in coming years. Factors that are causing loss of jobs include the low cost and ready availability of factory-made clothing and the invention of labor-saving machinery such as computerized sewing and cutting machines. In fact, automated machines are expected to replace many sewing jobs in the next decade. In addition, the apparel industry has declined in this country as many businesses choose to produce their items abroad. In these countries, workers are paid less and working conditions are often unregulated.

Tailors and dressmakers who do reliable and skillful work, however, particularly in the areas of mending and alterations, should be able to find employment. This industry is large, employing thousands of people. Many job openings will be created as current employees leave the workforce due to retirement or other reasons.

Glossary

accredited approved as meeting established standards for providing good training and education; this approval is usually given by an independent organization of professionals

annual salary the money an individual earns for an entire year of work

apprentice a person who is learning a trade by working under the supervision of a skilled worker; apprentices often receive classroom instruction in addition to their supervised practical experience

associate's degree an academic rank or title granted by a community or junior college or similar institution to graduates of a two-year program of education beyond high school

bachelor's degree an academic rank or title given to a person who has completed a four-year program of study at a college or university; also called an undergraduate degree or baccalaureate

bonus an award of money in addition to one's typical salary that is given to an employee for extra-special work or achievement on the job

career an occupation for which a worker receives training and has an opportunity for advancement

certified approved as meeting established requirements for skill, knowledge, and experience in a particular field; people are certified by an organization of professionals in their field

college a higher education institution that is above the high school level

community college a public or private two-year college attended by students who do not usually live at the college; graduates of a community college receive an associate's degree and may transfer to a four-year college or university to complete a bachelor's degree

diploma a certificate or document given by a school to show that a person has completed a course or has graduated from the school

distance education   a type of educational program that allows students to take classes and complete their education by mail or the Internet

doctorate   the highest academic rank or title granted by a graduate school to a person who has completed a two- to three-year program after having received a master's degree

fellowship   a financial award given for research projects or dissertation assistance; fellowships are commonly offered at the graduate, postgraduate, or doctoral levels

freelancer   a worker who is not a regular employee of a company; they work for themselves and do not receive a regular paycheck

fringe benefit   a payment or benefit to an employee in addition to regular wages or salary; examples of fringe benefits include a pension, a paid vacation, and health or life insurance

graduate school   a school that people may attend after they have received their bachelor's degree; people who complete an educational program at a graduate school earn a master's degree or a doctorate

intern   an advanced student (usually one with at least some college training) in a professional field who is employed in a job that is intended to provide supervised practical experience for the student

internship   1. the position or job of an intern; 2. the period of time when a person is an intern

junior college   a two-year college that offers courses like those in the first half of a four-year college program; graduates of a junior college usually receive an associate's degree and may transfer to a four-year college or university to complete a bachelor's degree

liberal arts   the subjects covered by college courses that develop broad general knowledge rather than specific occupational skills; the liberal arts are often considered to include philosophy, literature and the arts, history, language, and some courses in the social sciences and natural sciences

major (in college)   the academic field in which a student specializes and receives a degree

master's degree   an academic rank or title granted by a graduate school to a person who has completed a one- or two-year program after having received a bachelor's degree

pension   an amount of money paid regularly by an employer to a former employee after he or she retires from working

scholarship   A gift of money to a student to help the student pay for further education

social studies   courses of study (such as civics, geography, and history) that deal with how human societies work

starting salary   salary paid to a newly hired employee; the starting salary is usually a smaller amount than is paid to a more experienced worker

technical college   a private or public college offering two- or four-year programs in technical subjects; technical colleges offer courses in both general and technical subjects and award associate's degrees and bachelor's degrees

undergraduate   a student at a college or university who has not yet received a degree

undergraduate degree   see bachelor's degree

union   an organization whose members are workers in a particular industry or company; the union works to gain better wages, benefits, and working conditions for its members; also called a labor union or trade union

vocational school   a public or private school that offers training in one or more skills or trades

wage   money that is paid in return for work done, especially money paid on the basis of the number of hours or days worked

Browse and Learn More

Books

Beker, Jeanne, and Nathalie Dion. *Passion for Fashion: Careers in Style.* Toronto, ON.: Tundra Books, 2008.

Bochner, Arthur. *The New Totally Awesome Money Book for Kids.* 3d ed. New York: Newmarket, 2007.

Cindrich, Sharon, and Shannon Laskey. *A Smart Girl's Guide to Style: How to Have Fun With Fashion, Shop Smart, and Let Your Personal Style Shine Through.* Middleton, Wisc.: Pleasant Company Publications, 2010.

Clay, Kathryn, and Julia Nielsen. *How to Draw Cool Fashions.* Bloomington, Ind.: Snap Books, 2009.

Cleeland, Holly. *Glue & Go Costumes for Kids: Super-Duper Designs with Everyday Materials.* New York: Sterling, 2006.

Clewer, Carolyne. *Kids Can Knit: Fun and Easy Projects for Small Knitters.* Hauppauge, N.Y.: Barron's Educational Series, 2003.

Daynes, Katie, Lesley Sims, and Nilesh Mistry. *The Fabulous Story of Fashion.* Atlanta, Ga.: Usborne Books, 2006.

Dunn, Mary R. *I Want to Be a Fashion Designer.* New York: PowerKids Press, 2008.

Dupernex, Alison. *Start to Knit.* Petaluma, Calif.: Search Press, 2009.

Falick, Melanie. *Kids Knitting: Projects for Kids of All Ages.* New York: Artisan, 2003.

Frings, Gini Stephens. *Fashion: From Concept to Consumer.* 9th ed. Upper Saddle River, N.J.: Prentice Hall, 2007.

Goss, Judy. *Break into Modeling for Under $20.* New York: St. Martin's Griffin, 2008.

Harman, Hollis Page. *Money Sense for Kids.* 2d ed. Hauppauge, N.Y.: Barron's Educational Series, 2005.

House, Deborah. *Quick Costumes for Kids: 30 Great Fancy Dress Ideas.* London, U.K.: Hamlyn, 2007.

Jones, Jen. *Fashion Modeling: Being Beautiful, Selling Clothes.* Mankato, Minn.: Capstone Press, 2007.

Lanza, Barbara. *Fashionable Fun: How to Draw Cool & Casual Fashions.* Mineola, N.Y.: Dover Publications, 2009.

McAlpine, Margaret. *Working in the Fashion Industry.* Strongsville, Ohio: Gareth Stevens Publishing, 2005.

Milligan, Lynda, and Nancy Smith. *The Best of Sewing Machine Fun For Kids.* Concord, Calif.: C&T Publishing, 2004.

———. *Sewing Fun for Kids: Patchwork, Gifts & More.* Concord, Calif.: C&T Publishing, 2006.

Muehlenhardt, Amy Bailey, and Bob Temple. *Drawing and Learning About Fashion.* Mankato, Minn.: Picture Window Books, 2005.

Pease, Pamela. *Design Dossier: The World of Design.* Chapel Hill, N.C.: Paintbox Press, 2009.

Platt, Richard. *They Wore What?!: The Weird History of Fashion & Beauty.* Lanham, Md.: Two-Can Publishing, 2007.

Press, Debbie. *Your Modeling Career: You Don't Have to Be a Superstar to Succeed.* 2d ed. New York: Allworth Press, 2004.

Rogers, Barb. *Costumes, Accessories, Props, and Stage Illusions.* Colorado Springs, Colo.: Meriwether Publishing, 2005.

———. *Instant Period Costume: How to Make Classic Costumes from Cast-Off Clothing.* Colorado Springs, Colo.: Meriwether Publishing, 2001.

Running Press. *Make It Work!: A Fashion Lover's Journal.* Philadelphia: Running Press Kids, 2010.

Ryan, Nellie. *Designer Doodles: Over 100 Designs to Complete and Create.* Philadelphia: Running Press Kids, 2009.

Sadler, Judy Ann, and Jane Kurisu. *Simply Sewing.* Tonawanda, N.Y.: Kids Can Press, 2004.

Sember, Brette McWhorter. *The Everything Kids' Money Book: Earn It, Save It, and Watch It Grow!* 2d ed. Cincinnati, Ohio: Adams Media Corporation, 2008.

Stalder, Erika. *Fashion 101: A Crash Course in Clothing.* San Francisco: Orange Avenue Publishing, 2008.

Teen Vogue. *The Teen Vogue Handbook.* New York: Razorbill, 2009.

Thompson, Lisa. *Trendsetter: Have You Got What It Takes to Be a Fashion Designer?* Mankato, Minn.: Compass Point Books, 2008.

Williams, Roshumba, and Anne Marie O'Connor. *The Complete Idiot's Guide to Being a Model.* 2d ed. New York: Alpha, 2007.

Periodicals

The Artisan
http://www.local706.org/artisan.cfm

CosmoGIRL!
http://www.seventeen.com/cosmogirl

The Costume Designer
http://www.costumedesignersguild.com/cdg-magazine

Display & Design Ideas Magazine
http://www.ddionline.com/displayanddesignideas/index.shtml

GQ
http://www.gq.com

Glamour
http://www.glamour.com

Harper's Bazaar
http://www.harpersbazaar.com

InStyle
http://www.instyle.com

The New York Times: Fashion & Style
http://www.nytimes.com/pages/fashion

Seventeen
http://www.seventeen.com

Teen Vogue
http://www.teenvogue.com

Time for Kids
http://www.timeforkids.com/TFK

W
http://www.wmagazine.com

Women's Wear Daily
http://www.wwd.com

Web Sites

American Library Association: Great Web Sites for Kids
http://www.ala.org/greatsites

Apparel Search Main Glossary
http://www.apparelsearch.com/glossary.htm

Career Threads.com
http://careerthreads.com

Costume Institute of the Metropolitan Museum of Art
http://www.metmuseum.org/Works_of_Art/department.asp?dep=8

Dress King Fashion Glossary
http://www.dressking.com/search/glossary.htm

Elle Girl
http://ellegirl.elle.com

FashionBook.com
http://fashionbook.com

FashionClub.com
http://www.fashionclub.com

Fashion-Era
http://www.fashion-era.com

Fashion Net: How to Become a Fashion Photographer
http://www.fashion.net/howto/fashionphotographer

Fashion-Schools.org
http://www.fashion-schools.org

Kohls.com Glossary of Fabric & Fashion Terms
http://www.kohlscorporation.com/ecom/valueadded/Glossary.htm

Museum at the Fashion Institute of Technology
http://fitnyc.edu/3662.asp

OnlineNewsHour Extra: Fashion Issue
http://www.pbs.org/newshour/on2/fashion.html

Retail Careers Center
http://www.nrffoundation.com/content/retail-careers-center

Style.com
http://www.style.com

Style.com: Fashion Shows
http://www.style.com/fashionshows

Index

746.92 F248   INFCW
Discovering careers.

CENTRAL LIBRARY
03/12